THE NEW BLACK WOMAN: UNLOCKING THE QUEEN WITHIN

ESCAPING THE MENTAL PRISON WITH POSITIVE AFFIRMATIONS

JT JENNINGS

CONTENTS

INTRODUCTION

"Don't wait around for other people to be happy for you. Any happiness you get you've got to make yourself."

— ALICE WALKER

"Do you agree with this book ... that babies are racist?" She was reasonably shocked. And then she paused for seven full seconds, which felt like a year in the sterile setting of the Senate judiciary committee. For the only time in the 13 hours of questioning that she endured that day, she was visibly thrown off.

Here she was, at the age of 51, with about ten years of experience as a federal judge behind her and, if she was confirmed, the history-making honor of becoming the first Black woman to sit on the country's highest court ahead of her. And someone asked her if babies were racist?!

After collecting herself, she calmly replied, "I don't believe that any child should be made to feel as though they are racist or not valued, or less than, that they are victims, oppressors," she said eventually. When the senator refused to drop the subject she decided to give him a more direct answer.

"I have not reviewed any of those books," she said. "They don't come up in my work as a judge, which I'm respectfully here to address."

Ketanji Brown Jackson, one of the most influential Black women in America, the first Black woman to become a supreme court justice in the United States of America, accomplished an amazing feat. But she endured many struggles and challenges to get to where she is today. If you watched the hearings during her confirmation, you saw how she was attacked and harassed by her Republican colleague, Ted Cruz. Even though she had an impeccable record and years of experience, she was being racially attacked by inappropriate questions designed to throw her into confusion and question her character.

Rightfully, several people were outraged. Raphael Warnock, the Democratic senator from Georgia, said in the New York Times: "Would they be asking these questions if this were not a Black woman?"

The answer is no. This wasn't the first time a Black woman has been patronized and undermined because of her skin color. It has been going on for decades. If a woman so accomplished, decorated, and qualified as Judge Ketanji Jackson Brown had to endure such scrutiny and questioning, what does that mean for the rest of us, Black women? How do we traverse our lives day to day with this kind of treatment?

Being a Black woman in today's world is challenging. It often feels like society is bent on molding us into different versions of ourselves, none of which is pleasant or true.

So what happens? We get pulled in so many directions until we end up on the ground, lost, confused, and far away from who we are. If you're reading this, you probably feel like you're not good enough at times. You try so hard to please everyone around you. You probably have dreams and goals you've abandoned because you believe you lack what it takes to achieve them. You have allowed yourself to believe that you're not good enough and incapable of doing anything worthwhile.

Maybe people around you have put you into that crazy Black woman stereotype, and you're starting to doubt yourself a little. I know the feeling because I have been there before and I know how hard it is to doubt yourself at every turn.

That's why I wrote this book. I'll show you how to love yourself completely and gain your self-confidence. You'll learn how to reject stereotypes and bask in the beauty of your uniqueness. You'll also learn how to develop a healthy mindset that will enable you to win in life, and lastly, you'll finally see the amazing riches you have as a beautiful, strong Black woman. And these will happen through the power of positive affirmations.

I'm a fellow Black woman who learned how to take back my power by changing my mindset. I learned how to embrace my identity as a Black woman with these affirmations. I have always been passionate about helping Black women develop a strong, healthy mindset and achieve their dreams and goals.

I know what it means to fight against discrimination, stereotypes, and prejudice. That's why I set up a non-profit organization that celebrates the beauty of Black hair. I dream that Black women all over the world learn how to love themselves completely and change their thinking and mindset.

Affirmations are powerful, and they can help you build a healthy mindset. Success and confidence start in the mind. So take this journey with me, and I assure you that you will have discovered amazing things about yourself by the time you get to the last page. These affirmations are meant to be a permanent part of your life, so don't hesitate to come back to them whenever you need to. So turn the page, and let's get started on this amazing journey!

"I need to see my beauty and to continue to be reminded that I am enough, that I am worthy of love without effort, that I am beautiful, that the texture of my hair and that the shape of my curves, the size of my lips, the color of my skin, and the feelings that I have are all worthy and okay."

— TRACIE ELLIS ROSS

1

TAKING CHARGE OF YOUR MORNING

"If you are always trying to be normal, you will never know how amazing you can be."

— MAYA ANGELOU

"Bzzz, bzz, bzz!" The blaring alarm from my phone startled me awake many a morning. It was a sound that I had grown to dread. It signaled the start of yet another day, and more often than not, a day like every other. Most mornings I felt a tinge of anxiety and stress, and I simply did not feel ready for the day ahead of me. Even once I managed to peel myself from the bed, I was accosted by the crust in my eyes and fearful of what lay underneath my bonnet. I hated the feeling of being assaulted by angst and a lack of motivation every morning. It almost felt crushing. And before I knew it, I had set the bar so low, that I had virtually no positive expectations for my day. Even if this doesn't describe you, we all have had those mornings that are a challenge, where the weight of life is already sitting on your shoulders. And to top this off, most of us know that how we start our morning determines the quality of our day. So how do we combat this?

I overcame this hurdle with positive affirmations, which have become an important part of my daily practice over the last few years. As mentioned before, your morning routine can have a big impact on how your day goes, especially if you're prone to negative self-talk from the moment you wake up. An effective technique to alter your focus is establishing a habit in which you begin each day by doing, thinking, or saying something nice.

It doesn't need to be anything elaborate. Affirmations are meant to be simple, basic, yet powerful phrases that enable your subconscious mind to assert something as true (like making your subconscious thoughts conscious). They're "I" statements or mantras that you say to yourself several times. Trust me when I say that you have no idea how positive affirmations can change your life for the better if you use them daily. Affirmations can help you shift into a calm frame of mind if you wake up feeling worried or your mornings are filled with dread.

Affirmations have been shown to influence the brain on a molecular level, implying that our beliefs are linked to our health. They can help you feel empowered, make you more conscious of your thoughts, and encourage you to surround yourself with things you enjoy. At first, they may feel...uncomfortable or unnatural and this is nothing to be ashamed of. It took a lot of practice before I got used to it. When you make affirmations a habit, you'll notice that you become more conscious of your self-doubt and negative thinking patterns as they begin to shift.

Mornings are perfect for affirmations since the negativity and tension of the previous day have passed. It's a fantastic time to remind yourself that the opportunities are unlimited and that there's something to look forward to every day of your life, regardless of your current situation.

Speaking positive affirmations early in the morning has the power to enhance and improve your life! I have written some of my favorite morning affirmations below. They're meant to inspire and encourage you, but I also want you to make up some of your own based on your needs and experiences. It covers several aspects of your life, but we'll get more specific in the next chapters.

I usually do this in front of a mirror because it's more effective and really gives me a sense of strength and courage. So, I recommend that you do the same.

So, when you wake up in the morning, look at yourself in the mirror and say these affirmations out loud:

❖ **Today, I wake up with joy and courage, ready to explore all the opportunities that come my way.**
❖ **I am full of energy and determination.**
❖ **My words are powerful and will have a great impact today.**
❖ **With these beautiful hands, I will do amazing things.**
❖ **I am prepared for what the day will bring.**
❖ **I refuse to be mediocre today.**
❖ **I choose to only dwell on positive thoughts.**
❖ **I can do so much more than I can imagine.**
❖ **I have the power to make my life anything I want it to be.**
❖ **I go forth and conquer today.**
❖ **I am not afraid of being myself.**
❖ **Today I will speak positivity to those around me.**
❖ **I will have a beautiful day.**

❖ I choose to be happy today.

❖ I am filled with joy and confidence.

❖ Today I am refreshed and renewed.

❖ I am here for a reason and today I will live out my purpose.

❖ Nothing can stop me from accomplishing my goals today.

❖ I am in charge of my emotions, and today I choose joy.

❖ I am destined for great things and today is the start.

❖ I have the wisdom to achieve anything I want.

❖ I am determined to accomplish anything I set my mind to.

❖ My dreams, experiences, and ambitions are valid.

❖ I live and dwell in abundance because my life is full of good things.

❖ I am whole and complete in myself.

❖ I deserve love, kindness, peace, and respect.

❖ Today, I choose to accept the things that I cannot control and correct the things I can.

❖ I am not afraid to step into the unknown.

❖ I say no to negativity and stereotypes. Societal labels do not define me.

❖ I am not afraid to leave my comfort zone and explore my many potentials.

❖ I am a walking expression of grace and peace.

❖ I am growing and evolving every day.

❖ Today I will learn something new and amazing about myself.

❖ I have so much love to give.

❖ I deserve only the best, and I will not settle for less.

❖ Today, I let my light shine brightly.

❖ I am a bonafide, strong, and beautiful Black woman.

❖ I work towards achieving my dreams.

❖ Today, I choose to live a life of purpose.

❖ I bring beauty, grace, and increase to anything I lay my hands on.

❖ I am not worried about anything.

❖ I walk into a room with confidence, knowing that I have so much to give.

❖ I embrace my strengths and weaknesses.

❖ I don't need to be like anyone else. I am special and unique.

❖ I don't need validation from people to feel good about myself.

❖ Today is a gift, and I will live it the best way I can.

❖ I embrace this phase of my life.

❖ I have what it takes to achieve my goals, and I achieve them.

❖ My dreams and ambitions are becoming a reality.

❖ I chase my goals with passion and determination.

❖ I am a multi-talented woman destined to impact my generation and the world.

❖ My ideas and opinions matter and I am not afraid to share them.

❖ Every day, I learn new things to improve myself and improve my career.

❖ I attract amazing opportunities every day.

❖ I am here to make a change.

❖ My presence makes a big difference.

❖ I belong in any room I walk into.

❖ I reject self-doubt and lack of confidence.

❖ Obstacles and challenges don't discourage me. I use them as stepping stones to greatness.

❖ I am resilient, organized, and productive in anything I do.

❖ Today is filled with glorious opportunities for me.

❖ I don't run away from success because I deserve it and can achieve it.

❖ I generate value every day.

❖ I inspire the people around me every day.

❖ My craft is worthy of acceptance and admiration.

❖ I am not afraid of criticism and rejection. They are like fuel on the fire that burns within me.

❖ My mistakes don't define me. I learn from them, and I become better.

❖ I am built for success.

❖ I have an amazing ability to overcome any challenge that confronts me.

❖ My future is bright and full of promise.

❖ Every day, I get closer to becoming the woman I'm meant to be.

❖ I am needed, I am wanted, and I am here to fulfill my purpose.

❖ I am a change agent. I set things in motion.

❖ I can achieve the impossible.

❖ I never give up; I stay grounded and focused until I achieve my goals.

❖ I am not fazed or offended by people's opinions of me.

❖ I know how to filter people's words as I take what's meant for me and discard the rest.

❖ I strive to be the best me that I can be.

❖ Every day is a fresh start for me.

❖ Today is filled with endless possibilities.

❖ I am equipped for what the day has to offer.

❖ I am emotionally and mentally prepared for what today will bring.

❖ I am strong enough to tackle the challenges throughout my day.

❖ I am grateful for another day of life.

❖ I will celebrate even the little victories throughout my day.

❖ I bring energy into every space I enter.

❖ I accept that I am only human and do the best that I can.

❖ I am not deterred by the challenges before me.

❖ Today I am stronger than yesterday, and I refuse to settle.

❖ Today I am excited to push my body and mind to new limits.

2

ADJUSTING YOUR CROWN

"Self-esteem comes from being able to define the world on your terms and refusing to abide by the judgments of others."

— OPRAH WINFREY

R emember one of those speeches Eli Pope gave Olivia Pope in the series *Scandal*? He told her that she had to do twice what "they" were doing to get to their position. And remember how he always went on about how he had to do so much more to get to where he was, while Fitz was served everything on a silver platter because he was a rich white male?

I'm sure there are times you've felt this way, though to a lesser degree. And honestly, I have too. There have been times in my life when I have struggled with low self-esteem and a lack of confidence. I wasn't comfortable in my skin and often felt like I had to do double what my peers were doing to get the same results. In fact, many Black women have been told that they must do more to be seen and heard as we are constantly being badgered to act in a certain way or speak in a certain manner to be valued.

But the truth is you can't go through life constantly trying to beat the competition. It's exhausting. I had to learn how to separate myself from the need to prove something to the world. I had dreams and goals I wanted to achieve, but I wanted to achieve them for myself and not make a statement.

There are times when we decide to do things to prove someone wrong, and it's completely understandable. The problem is that as we live our lives in that mindset, it slowly but steadily chips away at our self-esteem and self-identity until we lose ourselves. We need to come to that point where we're at peace and confident in who we are, devoid of societal labels and expectations. I mean, Black women have heard it all. We've been called many things, from the famous "angry Black woman" to "mammies," "welfare queens," "baby mamas," and "smiling Aunt Jemima's."

But a time will come when you have to get rid of those stereotypes and create your identity. To do this, you have to embrace your weaknesses and your strengths. You have to decide to be true to yourself no matter what, no matter how much society tells you to be something else. You have to own all your flaws and quirks.

I know many of us struggle with imposter syndrome and believe that we don't deserve as much as the next person. We have to get rid of that mindset and fearlessly pursue our dreams. It took a long time for me to get to that point, but I can tell you that it's worth it.

Once I had healthier self-esteem, I realized that knowing my worth led me to set more realistic goals for myself rather than striving for perfection. Similarly, I was able to maintain a positive attitude when life threw me curveballs. I could finally trust in my abilities and as a result, became more adaptable to the unpredictability of life. All of this can be possible for you as well, just take it one step at a time.

Here's a poem I wrote when I was in a tough season in my life. I was struggling to get out of the people-pleasing web I was so engrossed in. I was learning how to brush off people's judgments without hardening my heart. I didn't want to build a wall around my heart and begin to distrust everyone; I wanted to live freely, and I hope it helps you regain the self-confidence you may have lost.

The Web

I wish the media didn't write my feelings,
I wish society would finally relinquish its talons from my soul,
I wish my thoughts weren't my greatest foe,
I wish my identity wasn't what I lacked and that it wasn't always that I was less than,
Many say, oh I know the trick, just stop caring about what others think of you,
But has anyone tried this?
Surely no one wants to be physically ostracized from society,
Is the life of an emotional hermit desirable,
I want so deeply to connect with others,
To connect with them in the raw essence of who I am,
But how can I?

The truth is, no matter how hard I try, I always lay up at night playing and replaying moments, actions, and feelings and can't stop obsessing over how people view me,
Their facial expressions, body language, words, and sounds,

spray from their being like tiny particles that land on the web
of my heart, stuck, trapped until I crawl onto the fragile web
and choose what to consume and what to leave behind,
Unfortunately for me, let's just say I never go hungry
Not a morsel goes to waste,
But I lay in waste,
And I see the effects around my waist,
I'm a little chubby,
Pumped with artificial favors, MSG AKA "mind searing
garbage," polyunsaturated gimmicks, "carboliedrates," and
about 3 grams of digest-it-all,
Just suppress-it-all, just depressed that's all,
Guess you can say I'm the whole package,
You can read me front or back,
Skim over my Nutrition Facts,
But wait, is this nutritional?
Certainly not medicinal like a puff on crack, like a haze, the
smoke clears, you're Black?
How do I react?
How do I project me without filtering it through the lens of he
or she
Where do you find contentment in self
when the world is supply and demand
when it supplies you lies packaged as truths that you didn't
even demand
Even if I write laws for my autonomy they're vetted before
they're passed

And I can't even look into the past cause it's all aghast
I just see that little chocolate girl staring back at the camera
with a lost look on her face
She's in the midst of understanding gender, even race
Little did she know she was in a race,
Competing for the end, for death...of self.

I can't close my eyes to the news, to the current events of my
world,
Because how can I connect if I don't know?
How can I commune if others can't find a semblance of like-
ness, of humanity in me
It's so hard to figure out who's me, who's she, who's I?

There's this dream I have of one day looking in the mirror
and seeing perfection and beauty,
Not just on a "good day" but every day
And not saying to myself, Oh good, I've finally outgrown this
or that,
But rather have grown to love the she in the mirror and the I
looking back

Perhaps it's just learning to leave more on the web,
Learning that I can in fact survive on less.
And my web will surely break under the load,
But it's OK; I have the tools, I'll build a new one at last,
One that congeals future, present, and past.

One that transcends corporeal limits and dimensions,
one not woven together by society,
but the fibers from within my soul.

If I could get through that challenging phase of my life and find out who I really am, then you can too.

To help you along the way, I have written some affirmations that allowed me to overcome low self-esteem and regain my confidence. As I said in the previous chapter, you must say these affirmations aloud and in front of a mirror.

So, as we did in the previous chapter, look at yourself in the mirror and say these affirmations out loud:

❖ **I value myself.**
❖ **I am worthy of the good that comes to me in life.**
❖ **My voice matters and needs to be heard.**
❖ **I have important thoughts, ideas, and perspectives to contribute.**
❖ **I am proud to be a Black woman.**
❖ **I am proud to be a part of the Black community.**
❖ **It's okay to love who I am now, even as I continue to evolve.**
❖ **I do not need to criticize someone else to elevate myself.**
❖ **I am worthy of all things wonderful.**

❖ I am in the exact place I need to be at this moment.

❖ I am grateful for all the good things happening in my life.

❖ I release all negative emotions and thoughts from my heart and mind.

❖ I deserve a life of love, peace, and happiness.

❖ I release all my worries and fears.

❖ I am content and at ease with who I am.

❖ I pursue peace and dwell on pleasant emotions.

❖ I focus my feelings and thoughts on happy experiences.

❖ I refuse to let the challenges I'm facing weigh me down because I know it's temporary.

❖ I focus on feelings of serenity, tranquility, and other pleasurable emotions.

❖ I am in control of my thoughts.

❖ I constantly walk in my power as a Black woman.

❖ I am in control of my life.

❖ I attract positive things to my life.

❖ I can handle any challenge that comes my way.

❖ I exhale fear and inhale confidence.

❖ I am completely accepting of myself.

❖ My strength is limitless.

❖ I am far more capable than I realize.

❖ I have earned the right to be good to myself.

❖ I take one step at a time.

❖ I am so proud of myself.

❖ I work on my weaknesses and build upon my strengths every day.

❖ I adore myself, quirks and all.

❖ I give myself space to heal.

❖ I am not perfect, but I'm a work in progress.

❖ I am becoming a better version of myself.

❖ I am self-sufficient and in command of my life.

❖ I am deserving of positive experiences.

❖ I accept myself completely.

❖ My uniqueness is a gift.

❖ I am strong and self-assured.

❖ I permit myself to be who I truly am.

❖ I am fortunate, loved, and cared for.

❖ I am more capable than I believe.

❖ I am secure and in command.

❖ I value my life and look for reasons to be grateful.

❖ I am capable of overcoming obstacles.

❖ I have faith in my ability to persevere in adversity.

❖ I believe in myself wholeheartedly.

❖ I treat myself with kindness and affection because I respect myself.

❖ Making mistakes is a natural part of life. They don't define me.

❖ I am deserving of the love and kindness that life has to offer.

❖ I am not my failures or mistakes.

❖ I let go of all kinds of self-doubt.

❖ My failures are accepted, but they do not
define me.

❖ I push through the hard days and look forward to
the brighter days ahead.

❖ My history has no bearing on my future.

❖ Even on the worst days, I keep hope in my heart.

❖ I strive to consistently better my life because I
believe I am deserving of excellence.

❖ No matter what life throws at me, I will persevere.

❖ I welcome constructive criticism as it helps me to
grow.

❖ I define my identity, not others.

❖ I am not a quitter.

❖ I do not allow the negativity of others to tear me
down.

❖ I have established boundaries that protect my
heart and mind.

❖ I refuse to quit on myself, even when life is hard.

❖ I love everything about myself and refuse to wear
a façade.

❖ The love I have for myself is limitless.

❖ I address negative feelings and replace them with
positive thoughts.

❖ I take pride in my efforts and celebrate my wins.

❖ I am not deterred by unwanted criticism.

❖ I refuse to stress about what others think of me.

* ❖ I will not be consumed by people's negative opinions.
* ❖ I am wonderfully unique, and I love who I am.
* ❖ I embrace positive thoughts about myself.
* ❖ I am rooted in self-love, and I can weather any storm.
* ❖ I let go of all emotions that are not beneficial to me.
* ❖ I have nothing to prove to anyone.
* ❖ I am one-of-a-kind and there is no one like me.
* ❖ My value is intrinsic.
* ❖ No one can set limits on my potential.
* ❖ I celebrate my individuality and take pride in who I am.
* ❖ My Blackness is lovable.
* ❖ I don't need to be perfect or flawless.

3

THE SUCCESSFUL BLACK WOMAN

"Know that you can start late, look different, be uncertain, and still succeed."

— MISTY COPELAND

The majority of your waking hours are spent working and more often than not, these are the prime years of your life. That said, you can't let work become your life. Whether you are an executive or flipping burgers, it is crucial to see yourself as more than your job and not let your job title define you. It's all too common for us to allow our bosses to dictate our happiness. We can put a lot of stock into whether we are given a promotion, selected for special projects, or acknowledged for our hard work.

However, with the right mindset, we can value our own efforts, speak out when necessary, or even leverage our skill sets to make an upward career move. We are not just who our bosses say we are; we can always strive for more.

I know many of us have experienced some sort of discrimination in the workplace. I have and it really hurts. Discrimination can especially come into play when it comes to negotiating salaries. Although sometimes we are jipped with our salaries because we have failed to do proper market research, oftentimes we simply accept lower pay because we either feel lucky to receive the amount offered or we are afraid to ask for more for fear of perhaps having the job offer rescinded altogether. But the thing is, we don't really want a lower pay. However, we expect it and don't question it. We've bought into that notion that we have to do more to get what other people are getting. Remember that scene in Scandal I talked about in the previous chapter? Eli Pope was telling Olivia how different she was from the people she was working with and how she had to do twice as much as they did to get to the top. It's been going on for years, and it's time we begin to demand what we deserve in the workplace.

Statistically, Black people going through the interview process assign themselves a lower numerical value of what they are worth as an employee or what the company has in the budget for that position.

I remember right after I graduated from college, I landed a job as a legal project assistant for a prestigious law firm. During the interview process, I was questioned extensively on my background, credentials, and experiences. In my heart, I knew I had crushed every answer. In my responses, I drew from my experiences as a juvenile defender in the county courts, my time as the president of the law club at my university, my summer internships for various law firms, and my graduating status of magna cum laude along with writing samples. By the second round of interviews, I knew the position was mine; I was confident. Despite being freshly out of college, I was well qualified for the position. However, once my offer letter finally came, it was far below what an associate legal assistant should make in the city of San Francisco. Nonetheless, I accepted the offer, no questions asked. Although I wish I could attribute this mistake to naivete, it wasn't that. I had somehow been deceived into believing that the offer reflected what I was worth. I went on to work under 12 attorneys, managed all aspects of the company's social media outlets, distilled thousands of pages of evidence, and went above and beyond the job description. But at the end of the day, I wasn't paid what I was worth.

This is why Black women need to gain the courage and awareness to fight for what they are worth and advocate for themselves.

Now let me share some affirmations that will help you change your perspective on your value in the workplace.

Remember how we've been doing it so far? Good. So, look in the mirror, stare at the beautiful woman you see, and repeat these affirmations aloud:

❖ **I can be an entrepreneur, create my own business, and grow wealth because I am creative, intelligent, and a boss.**
❖ **I am not afraid of hard work.**
❖ **I am deserving of promotions because I work hard, and I outperform my peers.**
❖ **I am deserving of a successful and fulfilling career.**
❖ **I am worth more than the offered pay, and I will negotiate until the offer reflects what I believe I am worth.**
❖ **My role is essential, and I am an impactful team player.**
❖ **I have all the things I need to succeed in my endeavors.**

❖ My talents are unique and valuable.

❖ I am a creative person.

❖ I am an astute individual.

❖ I am deserving of my current position.

❖ Every day, I look forward to learning something new.

❖ Any notion that comes to mind becomes a reality for me.

❖ I belong in my chosen career.

❖ My ideas are one-of-a-kind.

❖ I am brave enough to accomplish everything I set my mind to.

❖ I am equipped with the resources I'll need to succeed.

❖ I am going to take advantage of every learning opportunity that comes my way.

❖ I am full of self-assurance and optimistic energy.

❖ I attract success and my future is filled with opportunities.

❖ I'm devoted to putting in the effort required to reach my objectives.

❖ I choose a life rich with variety and optimism.

❖ I put everything I have into myself and my creative process.

❖ My job has a positive impact.

❖ I have all the qualities it takes to be a boss.

❖ With my positive energy, I attract like-minded people and clients.

❖ My desire to achieve my goal is fueled by my passion.

❖ I am a successful and intelligent person.

❖ Every day, I invest in myself and my company.

❖ I am full of talent and my imagination will take me far in business.

❖ I am pleased with myself and my achievements.

❖ I have faith in my chosen career path.

❖ I work hard and deserve to see positive results.

❖ As a learning tool, I embrace imperfection.

❖ I celebrate every win in the workplace no matter how small it seems.

❖ I am capable of completing difficult tasks at work.

❖ I am designing the life I want.

❖ I surround myself with mentors who are invested in my career development.

❖ I am good at balancing my priorities.

❖ What I can accomplish has no bounds.

❖ I have no fear of making mistakes on the job.

❖ I have respect for my career goals.

❖ My investments are returned to me and multiplied.

❖ I am creating wealth through my career.

❖ I make money through my knowledge.

❖ I concentrate my efforts on the important things.

❖ In my environment, I have a beneficial impact.

❖ I am highly competent at what I do.

❖ I let go of things that I can't control.

❖ I am not afraid to say no to my colleagues and boss.

❖ I am completely confident in my abilities.

❖ I take things at my own pace.

❖ Others value what I bring to the table.

❖ I am fine with taking things one step at a time.

❖ I attract people who will assist me in achieving my objectives.

❖ My concept of success is unique to me.

❖ The expectations of others do not define me.

❖ My career has no dead ends.

❖ If I am unhappy in my job, I am deserving of a better opportunity.

❖ I am not ashamed of transitions in my career or gaps in my resume.

❖ Challenges are there for my growth.

❖ Success and growth are what drive me.

❖ I am well-organized and efficient.

❖ I am proficient in my position.

❖ I am capable of solving difficult challenges.

❖ This is something I was born to do.

❖ I am confident in my talents.

❖ I am certain that I'm on the correct path.

❖ I add significance to the world.

❖ I am contributing to society, despite how others perceive my role.

❖ I am building my brand daily.

❖ Obstacles become opportunities for me.

❖ Challenges energize me.

❖ I am fully capable of running a business.

❖ My perseverance pays off.

❖ Others look up to me as an example.

❖ I am not going to give up.

❖ I am bursting with innovative ideas.

❖ My voice should be heard.

❖ I am entitled to a place at the table.

❖ My work is liked and respected.

❖ I am worth the money I ask for.

❖ I've got everything I'll need to get where I'm going.

❖ I refuse to compare my success. My journey is unique.

❖ My female perspective is wanted and needed.

❖ I create opportunities for my strengths to be seen.

❖ I readily share my talents in the workplace.

❖ My weaknesses are temporary and provide direction for my development.

❖ I am perfectly aligned with my purpose in life.

❖ I create solutions to difficult problems on the job.

❖ I expand my network and increase my opportunities for success.

❖ I am designed for greatness and refuse to accept mediocrity.

❖ I am committed to my vision of success.

❖ I have healthy boundaries between home and work.

❖ I embrace leaving my comfort zone to further develop myself.

4

TREAT THAT BANGING BODY RIGHT!

"Take care of your body. It is the only place you have to live."

— JIM ROHN

B lack women are blessed with banging bodies. I mean, when you look at women like Bianca Belair, Naomi (of WWE fame), and Serena Williams, you just know that we are truly blessed. These women, though beautiful, know the importance of prioritizing self-care and fitness. They are confident in their beauty, but they know how much care goes into having a healthy body and mind.

Who doesn't want to have a fit, sexy body? Everyone, right? But not all of us are willing to put in the work. It's crazy how much we underestimate the power of small lifestyle changes like exercise and a healthy diet.

It might not seem like a big deal but having a good diet will not only make you love what you see in the mirror, but it can also alter the chemical makeup of your brain.

As Black women living in America, most of us are used to eating the basic "American diet" which is mostly easy-make. These ready-to-go foods like burgers, pizza, wings, and pasta are extremely high in carbs. These foods spike your blood sugar, can alter your mood, disrupt your hormones, and even increase anxiety or hyperactivity.

When we feed our bodies healthy and nourishing foods, we are also feeding our minds. There's an adage that says, "trash in, trash out." And ain't this the truth? Your body is an incredibly complex system that has the capability of healing itself, creating life, and even performing amazing Olympic feats. On the other hand, your mind has the power to do everything from creating beautiful pieces of art to intricate computer code. But the question is, what will you feed it? How will you fuel this divine vessel you live within? I'm not telling you to give up all foods that bring you joy and turn into a gym rat. I just want you to see the need to create a healthier and more sustainable relationship with both food and fitness.

When I started eating right and exercising, I felt amazing! I felt so much better than I had in years. If you're wondering why you're always tired and struggling with low energy, your diet may be the culprit. Try changing your diet and incorporating exercise into your daily routine.

You don't have to start with major changes or drastic shifts in living. You can start with something as little as removing soda from your diet for a month. Or going on a 30-day no sugar challenge. There are countless ways to get more active such as walking your dog or picking up a new sport. Trust me when I say the results are totally worth it.

Now I know starting is usually the most difficult part, and there are times you'll feel like giving up. So here are some affirmations that will help you remain consistent. The key to staying motivated in anything is to constantly remind yourself why you're doing whatever it is you're doing.

So, just before you start your day, look at yourself in the mirror and repeat these affirmations aloud:

❖ The foods I am eating now lead to a better version of me.

❖ I have the willpower to say no when I am full.

❖ I have enough self-control to say no to unhealthy foods.

❖ Continued healthy eating will keep me looking and feeling well.

❖ I choose foods that are the building blocks for longer life.

❖ I feel great when I eat well.

❖ I have balance with my healthy eating.

❖ Cooking healthy meals is not hard.

❖ My body can trust me to prepare healthy meals.

❖ I am so much more than a diet or a number on the scale.

❖ I love planning healthy meals.

❖ I feel amazing when I eat healthy foods.

❖ I choose to replace junk food with healthy snacks.

❖ I am committed to a healthy eating lifestyle.

❖ I have discipline in my eating habits.

❖ I stop eating when my body signals I am full.

❖ I can decline food even if it offends others.

❖ I eat portions that are appropriate for my body.

❖ I derive energy from the healthy foods I eat.

❖ I ensure my body gets nourished from the foods I consume.

❖ I give my body the best foods.

❖ **Good health is my reward for healthy eating.**

Now, the next set of affirmations can be said just before you work out so you can stay motivated.

So, just before you start your daily workout routine, repeat these affirmations aloud:

❖ **I will have an excellent workout today.**
❖ **Today, my body will become stronger.**
❖ **I have the willpower to complete my exercise routine.**
❖ **I am strong and can do any exercise I want.**
❖ **The more I move my body, the more in sync my systems become.**
❖ **I take pleasure in exercising both my mind and body.**
❖ **When I make time for self-care, my body and mind thank me.**
❖ **I take care of myself so that I can take care of others.**
❖ **I will only consume content that is beneficial for my mental health.**
❖ **I will listen to my body when it feels off or tells me to slow down. I am worthy of rest.**
❖ **I enjoy working out at the gym.**
❖ **All of my workouts are purposeful and meaningful.**

❖ Going to the gym is exciting and challenging.

❖ My body is a strong machine.

❖ I've made the gym one of my favorite spots.

❖ I feel alive when I work out.

❖ I'm looking forward to going to the gym today.

❖ My body is capable of amazing things.

❖ I've made working out a habit.

❖ My body deserves to be taken care of.

❖ Hitting the gym makes me feel good and keeps me healthy.

❖ Working out relieves my anxiety and stress.

❖ I'm pleased with myself for working out regularly.

❖ I am motivated to keep my body strong and fit.

❖ Exercising gives me amazing energy.

❖ I enjoy my fitness routine.

❖ I'm getting stronger and fitter every day.

❖ I always find the time for exercise.

❖ As a result of my workout, my physical health and mood have improved.

❖ I am changing my body into the figure I've always desired.

❖ I feel confident in my health and wellness goals.

❖ I'm committed to strengthening my body.

❖ My muscles are tough and tenacious.

❖ Every day, I am becoming more and more powerful.

❖ My body is my home, and I give it the best possible care.

❖ I enjoy sculpting the body I've always desired.

❖ To me, having a strong body is crucial.

❖ I am committed to achieving my fitness goals.

❖ I am resolved never to give up until I achieve my objectives.

❖ Any goal I set for myself is within my reach.

❖ I am a strong, self-assured, and motivated individual.

❖ I'm proud of myself for making it this far.

❖ I have a lot of energy and am in fantastic health.

❖ My body and I are entirely in sync.

❖ I enjoy the way I feel after a good workout.

❖ Every time I sweat, I release poisons.

❖ Every morning, I am energized and ready to begin my fitness routine.

❖ Every day, my muscles grow stronger and provide me with more stamina.

❖ Exercising has improved my breathing and sleep.

❖ I'm grateful for a healthy physique that allows me to accomplish the things I want to do.

❖ Every day, I look forward to pushing my body to new limits.

❖ I am inspired to have a more active lifestyle.

❖ Pain is good because it reminds me that my muscles are growing and getting stronger.

❖ I enjoy going to different gym classes to work on different body parts.

❖ When possible, I walk instead of driving.

❖ Working out helps me to manage my stress and anxiety.

❖ I'm not someone who gives up easily.

❖ I've established weekly weight and cardio goals for myself, and I expect to meet them.

❖ I am devoted to giving it my all during my workouts.

❖ I am entirely committed because I know that hard work pays rewards.

❖ I take days off from exercising to avoid being over-worked and giving up.

❖ I am entitled to happiness and health.

❖ I care enough about myself to take better care of it.

❖ Every day, I'm making progress toward better health.

❖ I can lead a healthy lifestyle and I will.

❖ I continue to be inspired to look after myself.

❖ To keep my physique fit and sexy, I must continue to exercise.

❖ I don't need a gym membership to be healthy.

❖ Working out at home is energizing and satisfying.

❖ I will engage in physical activities that I enjoy.

❖ I will create a space in my home for physical activity.

❖ My diet compliments my physical activity and lifestyle.

❖ I don't have to be at the gym to get a good workout.

❖ Being active outdoors refreshes and recharges me.

❖ I enjoy swimming, hiking, and dancing because they give my body healthy movement.

❖ I will inspire my family to adopt a healthy lifestyle.

5

BLACK AND DROP-DEAD GORGEOUS

"We must cease being participants in our own oppression"

— STACEY ABRAMS

I know many of us are familiar with the reality TV show, America's Next Top Model. The show's host, popular Black supermodel Tyra Banks, said she started the competition to encourage young Black women to pursue their dreams and rise above the discrimination of Eurocentric beauty standards in the modeling industry.

But somehow, in the show, it seems some Black women were being asked to alter certain things about their complexion and hair. I guess it's all part of the business but I'm sure many of us found it awkward and distasteful. It's completely understandable. Why? Because it hurts to have to change who we are to fit societal standards. Beauty has always been a touchy subject for women, especially Black women. We love being beautiful, we love being called beautiful, but sadly, Black women have had to change practically everything about themselves to be deemed beautiful.

For many years Black women have had to deal with Eurocentric beauty standards. These standards have shaped how Black women view themselves, which is in sharp contrast to the beauty of a Black woman. This conflict is what creates such inner turmoil within Black women of all ages as they can never truly reach societal beauty standards. The essence of Black beauty is rooted in finding pride in every aspect of who you are, whether it is cultivated or God-given.

Let's talk about Black hair. But first, let's take a short trip back in time to see how much beauty and heritage is behind our thick coily mane.

Hair was a sacred cultural and spiritual symbol in ancient African societies. Throughout history, Black hair has been a representation of survival, resistance, and celebration.

[1]Braids were used as a tool for slaves looking to escape to freedom. Because drawing or writing directions was risky (and often difficult with little to no education), they would cornrow their hair to map escape routes, braiding the plaits into patterns that resembled roads to travel or avoid. Small bits of gold and seeds were hidden in the braids to sustain them after their escape.

That's why many Black women slaves made cornrows and other similar hairstyles. But after the abolition of slavery, Black hair seemed to have lost its beauty. It became a symbol of oppression, and straight, flat hair became the standard as Black women began to straighten their hair with relaxers.

My personal hair journey has had many ups, downs, twists, and turns. I started using relaxers at a young age. In fact, I only started growing my natural hair about 7 years ago. Throughout my childhood and teens, I felt that my natural hair wasn't pretty. It was thick and tightly coiled and whenever I started to sprout new growth, I would quickly apply relaxers to it. I thought my hair was more beautiful that way. I had the belief that my hair in its natural state was a chore, a hassle, and something only meant to be tamed. I felt that if my hair wasn't either permed, pressed, flat ironed, or at the very least slicked down with gel and edge control that it wasn't presentable for the outside world.

Once I reached college, I decided to grow out my natural hair and I fell madly in love with it. I did the big chop and snipped all of my processed strands. I didn't know my hair could be so strong and beautiful; I loved the way it formed little tendrils once I applied water and hair butters. I loved how versatile and resilient it was and how many different styles I could do with it. I couldn't believe that I no longer had to run from the rain, or humidity, or triple wrap my hair, shower cap and all, for fear that it would revert. My hair was amazing! And now, after growing my natural hair for many years, I can say that it's one of the best decisions I've ever made. Why did we ever believe that our natural hair was anything but beautiful?

What about our skin? Starting from the inception of colonization, Black people were viewed as ugly because of their rich Black skin. White or olive skin was seen as the perfect skin color. Throughout the African diaspora, it's sad that lots of beautiful women have begun to bleach their skin, not minding the consequences as they use treatments ranging from lightening soaps to skin peels.

I have always admired the beauty of Black skin and I am grateful for women like Viola Davis, Jennifer

Hudson, Kelly Rowland, Issa Rae, Lupita Nyong'o, and Tika Sumpter who have risen above the Eurocentric standard of beauty and embraced their gorgeous Black skin, especially in industries that don't always celebrate darker complexions.

Listen, Sis, we are beautiful beyond comparison. We are melanin goddesses, and we have to embrace the gift of our beautiful hair and skin. Here's a short poem I wrote a while back as I wrestled with the reprogramming of my own perception of beauty. It was written from the perspective of Eurocentrism as I attempted to articulate my frustrations with the societal pressures. Specifically, throughout our time in America, we have made many modifications to how we wear our hair. At times this was due to us trying to increase employability, but more often than not, we have pined after this golden standard of Western beauty. With each hairstyle change, it has affected our identity as a community. While our hair has been a symbol of power such as in the civil rights era, it has also been a source of shame for what grows naturally from our scalps. I entitled the poem "Spell" because I believe that many of us have been put under a spell, that tells us we must look a certain way to be seen as beautiful.

Spell

I put a spell on you
And you want nothing more than to look like me
You want to assimilate into the American Dream
Into the American way

Your hair has natural tendrils, locks, curls, and waves
So you bring out the heat

The searing hot comb, searing hair and consciences,
The flattening flat iron, flattening hair and egos

You bring out perms and relaxers, also known as hair crack
Cause you're addicted to its relaxing qualities, relaxing hair,
and standards
Permanently destroying self-worth

You wear silky straight wigs manufactured from plastic
factories
Willfully hiding the real you and then you wonder why
you're wiggin out

You sew in stitches and tracks of hair, not yours
so as not to leave a track leading towards your identity
which is wounded and treated by 5 rows of stitches

And then you pat it!
Oh no, you wouldn't want to disrupt the artificial terrestrial
landscape sitting atop your scalp
A woman's hair is her glory
But your hair is your scorn, see
I've put a spell on you...

The goal of this poem is not meant to shame any of us that choose to utilize various hair treatments and styles like perms, weaves, and wigs. Black hair is not one-dimensional. It doesn't matter if you bought it, installed it, glued it, or grew it. A Queen sets her own standard of beauty and should never be subjugated to someone else's. Don't succumb to the spell of society luring you to look a certain way to feel beautiful. Take off the veil from your eyes and snap out of the spell they try to put on us.

Now that you know just how amazingly stunning you are, let me share some affirmations that will help you develop a strong conviction about your uniqueness.

I have divided this section into hair and skin affirmations.

So here are some great hair affirmations. You know the drill. Look into the mirror and while touching your hair, say these words aloud. You can even say them while you go about your hair routine. I want you to make contact with your hair as you say these words:

❖ **The length of my hair does not determine its beauty.**

❖ **I am happy with my hair regardless of where it falls on a hair chart.**

❖ **I adore my crown in all of its uniqueness and glory.**

❖ **My crown tells a story.**

❖ **My beauty is so much more than my hair.**

❖ **How I wear my hair is my decision, and it is mine whether it grows from my head, or I purchase it.**

❖ **My hair is always beautiful.**

❖ **My hair is still lovely, curls or no curls.**

❖ **Every day, I take great care of my hair.**

❖ **It does not have to be difficult for me to grow my hair.**

❖ **I am self-assured enough to wear any hairstyle I like.**

❖ **I'm doing and will keep doing whatever it takes to make my hair happy.**

❖ **My hair growth and quality are both enough.**

❖ **My hair makes me joyful.**

❖ **My natural hair journey has been and will continue to be a success for me.**

❖ I'm still learning about hair and will keep doing so.

❖ My hair is something I treasure.

❖ My hair is not a burden.

❖ I can have whatever hairstyle I want, and I love it.

❖ I don't have bad hair, have never had bad hair, and will never have bad hair.

❖ I have realistic expectations for my hair.

❖ My hair and skin are both beautiful to me.

❖ My hair is one of my favorite features.

❖ My hair is something I'll always be grateful for.

❖ I'll always admire my hair.

❖ I shall refrain from using harmful products on my hair.

❖ I'll keep nourishing and respecting my hair.

❖ I will continue encouraging other Black women to love their skin and hair.

❖ I have a healthy relationship with my hair.

❖ The shape of my head is stunning.

❖ I'm going to make hair care simple, enjoyable, and low-effort.

❖ I'm not going to let other people's negativity affect me.

❖ I'm not going to compare my hair to other people's.

❖ I shall not harm my hair in the future.

❖ I'll get to my desired hair length.

❖ I will always take good care of my hair.

❖ My curl pattern is stunning.

❖ I can regrow my edges.

❖ My hair adds to my attractiveness.

❖ My hair is stunning in its natural state.

❖ My hair is deserving of praise and celebration.

❖ My hair suits me perfectly.

❖ Whether it's long, short, or medium length, my hair looks great.

❖ My hair was never unattractive. It has always been lovely.

❖ My bad hair habits will not be repeated in the future.

❖ My hair care products nourish my scalp and skin.

❖ This world will not suffocate and mute the originality of my hair.

❖ Hair or no hair, I am stunning.

❖ My hair does not define me.

❖ My gray hairs represent dignity and wisdom.

❖ There is nothing wrong with my hairline.

❖ My forehead is the perfect size.

Now, these are skin and body affirmations. You can say them while looking in the mirror, but I'd prefer you also say them while you're doing your skincare routine or getting dressed in the morning. Say to yourself:

❖ The melanin in my skin is divinely given, and its richness reflects my inner being.

❖ My skin is never too dark.

❖ My eyes are the perfect color.

❖ My skin does not have to be blemish-free to be beautiful.

❖ Makeup only accentuates my beauty. It does not create it.

❖ My nose and lips are a perfect size.

❖ All of my facial features are in the correct proportions.

❖ I am happy with my body.

❖ I have the perfect shape.

❖ I love my body because it functions.

❖ I am beautiful no matter what I wear. Brands and fashion trends do not define me.

❖ I will not be enslaved to vanity.

❖ I am sexy, and I revel in my femininity.

❖ My beauty is incomparable because no one is like me.

❖ My body is not to be fetishized or demeaned. My beauty is to be respected.

❖ I am beautiful and fully deserving of love.

❖ I will engage in the praising of my Black sisters' beauty.

❖ I am secure in how I present myself to the world.

❖ I really like what I see when I look in the mirror.

❖ My body is a gift, deserving of love and care.

❖ My stretch marks are beautiful and a part of my story.

❖ The number on the scale is arbitrary. How I feel is what's most important.

❖ I refuse to compare my body to another woman's. My body is unique.

❖ I accept that the images in magazines are photoshopped and airbrushed. They do not reflect reality.

❖ I am proud of all that my body has done.

❖ I have accomplished a lot with my body.

❖ I am aging beautifully.

❖ I am whole whether I am skinny or fat.

❖ I am desirable.

❖ I have the perfect amount of curves.

❖ I radiate beauty from head to toe.

❖ I walk with grace and my head held high.

❖ I appreciate every aspect of my body.

❖ The scars on my body are not mistakes, they are simply a part of my story.

❖ I am a vision of Black beauty.

❖ My pregnancy marks are nothing to be ashamed of. They represent my body's willingness to accommodate new life.

❖ My beauty does not fade with age or time.

❖ I am content with my curves.

❖ I do not fear the scale.

❖ My beauty needs no corrective surgery since there is nothing to fix.

6

GET THAT COIN

"One thing that's true is that whether you are making a financial investment or an investment of the heart, you usually get what you give. What's also true is that investing the wrong assets into the wrong places is a great way to end up broke (or broken)."

— DR. BOYCE WATKINS

Our finances are one of the most important aspects of life. It's one thing that boosts our self-worth and quality of our lives, especially as Black women. But this is also one of the areas where a majority of Black people are sadly disadvantaged. For centuries, Black people have been disadvantaged when it comes to generating wealth, and it's understandable as we haven't always had access to equal opportunities to create financial security.

An evaluation of wealth in the U.S. revealed evidence of extreme racial disparities. [1]In 2019 the average white household held $188,200 in wealth. This is 7.8 times that of the typical Black household $24,100. The current Black-white wealth gap is a direct result of decades-long trends in wealth inequality. For the past 30 years, the average wealth of white families has consistently dwarfed that of Black families—ranging from a gap of $106,900 in 1992 to $185,400 in 2007 (both adjusted for inflation to 2019 dollars).

These gaps in wealth between Black and white families show the devastating effects of years of inequality and discrimination. It also shows the differences in power and opportunity that can be traced back to this nation's inception. For example, the educational system in underprivileged communities isn't the same. Our grandparents weren't taught about appreciating and depreciating assets and starting a business. As a result, we were taught how to follow directions and settle for any job that could provide for our families.

So you see, the odds seem to be stacked against us. It's as though Black people are not supposed to be wealthy.

Remember the incident in January 2022 with Black Panther's director Ryan Coogler? He was judged by his appearance and treated like a criminal. He went to the bank to withdraw a few thousand dollars, and the tellers literally thought he wanted to rob the bank. It's as if they couldn't fathom a young Black man having the ability to withdraw even a few thousand dollars. Just because we are racially and historically disadvantaged, it doesn't mean it can't change. The situation will only stay the same if we don't do anything about it. This is where changing our mindset about money comes in.

When I was growing up, my parents were in the ministry. Although they had humble salaries, they taught me the importance of stretching every dollar you earn. In middle school, I badly wanted a pair of Chuck Taylors as they were the most popular shoes at the time. My parents couldn't afford to purchase a new pair. However, on one of our frequent trips to the thrift store, I found the cutest pink and black converse in my size. I begged my mom for the seven-dollar pair of shoes and excitedly went home to hand-wash the shoelaces and soles. The next day at school, I received so many compliments on my shoes because they were unique, and no one could seem to find the same ones I had. It was at that moment that I realized you didn't need to be rich to have an enviable wardrobe. I knew moving forward that secondhand didn't mean second class. The same thought process has carried on throughout my life, and I still live by it today.

Whether it's a new lace front, designer purse, shoes, or jewelry, there's always a new shiny object to pursue to achieve "that look." The question I continue to ask myself is if what I am going to purchase is a need or a want.

Trust me, I get it. I want the dream life I see on TV and Instagram too. I want a big house, a nice car, and a closet full of designer clothes, but due to the mindset and values that my parents instilled in me, I won't sabotage my financial future by living frivolously in the moment.

Writing this makes me remember one of Kendrick Lamar's songs entitled "Vanity Slaves." He talked about how much financial insecurity is prevalent in the Black community and its effect on our people. Let me share a few parts of the song that really hit home:

"The high school female needs earrings and details, so she can be cool to be, amongst popularity. The various name brands that reached the price scan. It's not about the right price but more like the right scam. To rule us

*all, confuse us all. Hit the bank within five minutes
and then withdraw. Now let's draw, the picture of a
rapper with a chain and Range that is not paid for.
My cousin from the South said he just bought him a
house that lives around his neck like a white collar. So
I fast forward, then I rewind a time machine can help
me double back to slavery times...Picking cotton from
a field that a white man own. The blacker you are,
farther you're from the white man's home. I said the
400 years we never had nothing. Barely had clothes on
our back. Is the reason why when we get a little bit of
change. We exaggerate on our living expenses."*

— KENDRICK LAMAR, VANITY SLAVES

Slavery was abolished, but many of us have become modern-day slaves, vanity slaves. We are obsessed with our vanity and pursue materialism to any end, as we still haven't gotten over it. Many will make the argument that we have been removed from slavery for many decades. However, throughout the course of our time in America, we have been oppressed. We not only experienced slavery, but also other forms of oppression ranging from police brutality to inequalities in the justice system. And although we are physically free, we have failed to liberate our minds. We've been told so frequently that we can never amount to anything and that we are worth nothing. So what do we do to satiate these feelings? We base our worth on the material things that we have been restricted from. Many of us don't feel good about ourselves unless we're wearing luxurious designer clothes and driving flashy cars. And even though we can't afford these expensive things that we don't necessarily need, we incur thousands in debt— such high levels of debt that keep us in a rat race, living paycheck to paycheck. The cycle continues generationally, and it must stop with us. We can regain our power!

I've learned not to allow material things to define my worth. Listen, Sis; you don't need to have a hundred Hermes Birkins in your closet to feel worth it. You don't need to own a dozen Louboutins. You don't need a new lace front every month or new acrylics and lashes every two weeks.

We can create generational wealth. All we have to do is change the way we think about money, and we have to reassess our money spending habits. Things like buying expensive items that don't appreciate in value, failing to save, impulsive spending, incurring bad debts, and not investing, will only keep us in the hole. We can teach our children to change the way they see their assets and material possessions. Money should be used as a tool for positive change and not as a symbol of self-worth or idolatry. That's how we break the cycle of financial slavery.

Now let's talk briefly about another limiting money mindset we need to address. It's called the scarcity mindset. If you live paycheck to paycheck, you've probably acquired a scarcity mindset when it comes to money. In addition, you may have experienced a life event that has altered your financial outlook. As a result, you're now operating from that mental space, which leads to less-than-ideal results.

You may be afraid of spending money, or you might spend the majority of it as soon as it appears in your account. While there are clearly emotional sides to this, the way you think about money and how you make and spend it is the most important. If you have a scarcity mindset, you'll find yourself constantly preoccupied with never having enough.

So, how can we go from scarcity to abundance?

With an abundance mindset, you can analyze every possible beneficial outcome for your financial situation while being open to them all. Because it is neither a choice nor something you stress about, the fear of wasting money or never having enough of it does not exist for you.

This is because, regardless of your financial circumstances, an abundance mindset states that you will always have more than you need to fulfill your goals. Your financial life will flow in the direction of the energy you give it once you start thinking like this. You will attain your goal if you focus on making and possessing more than enough money. But if you always focus on scarcity and lack, that will be your only experience with money.

This is where affirmations come in. The truth is, if you don't get rid of negative mindsets about your finances, you won't achieve your financial goals. So here are some of my favorite finance affirmations. These will reprogram your thinking and catapult you into a new mind frame of living with financial responsibility and a healthier relationship with money.

We're going to say them aloud like we've been doing:

❖ **I deserve financial freedom.**
❖ **I will manage my finances wisely.**
❖ **I am the steward of my wealth.**
❖ **I am purposeful with every dollar.**
❖ **The amount in my bank account does not define me.**
❖ **I attract wealth.**
❖ **I work hard for every cent I earn.**

❖ I am proud of my financial gains.

❖ Incremental growth is how I will develop wealth.

❖ I make smart financial decisions today, which will lead to wealth in my future.

❖ I will save for my future.

❖ I am creating generational wealth.

❖ I instill financial wisdom into those around me.

❖ I celebrate every dollar I earn as it provides for my family.

❖ I have a healthy view of money.

❖ My wealth is not just measured monetarily. My access to resources is just as important.

❖ I say no to things I don't need.

❖ My financial future is bright.

❖ I have a vision and a plan for the future of my finances.

❖ Abundance is coming. I will open my mind to new opportunities.

❖ Every dollar is accounted for.

❖ I respect my hard work. Therefore, I do not lend to people who have no true intention of paying me back.

❖ Money is a resource that has the potential to improve my life.

❖ I'm breaking generational curses.

❖ My background doesn't define my ability to create generational wealth.

❖ I am in charge of my finances; my finances are not in charge of me.

❖ I can make a better life for myself and my family.

❖ I am not concerned about my finances because I budget wisely.

❖ I am a competent woman who can overcome any financial challenge.

❖ I am not disadvantaged; I am on my way to being affluent.

❖ I will improve my financial situation.

❖ I have a lot of riches in my life that aren't monetary.

❖ I am confident in my capacity to manage the money that comes into my life.

❖ I am achieving my financial objectives.

❖ I can create the financial picture I want with determination and imagination.

❖ My income surpasses my expenses.

❖ My earning potential is limitless.

❖ My hard work yields wealth.

❖ I can use my abilities to create wealth.

❖ I am confident in my abilities to increase my earnings.

❖ In my life, there are numerous options to make extra money.

❖ I am entitled to the option of negotiating my compensation.

❖ I will leave a home for my children.

❖ I can use the money I earn to impact people and change the world.

❖ I have enough money to live comfortably in my daily existence.

❖ With enough time, I shall amass all of the riches I desire.

❖ I am on my path to being a millionaire.

❖ I am not going to let my current financial circumstances detract from my plans for the future.

❖ I am destined for greatness.

❖ I am entitled to all I desire in life.

❖ I attract wealth, happiness, and success.

❖ I have earned the right to leave a financial legacy for myself and my family.

❖ I am going to pay off all of my debts.

❖ My financial situation does not define me.

❖ Money will open more doors and provide more options for a comfortable life.

❖ I will stick to a budget.

❖ I will investigate multiple options for investing my money.

❖ I can make any amount of money I want.

❖ I diligently track all of my expenditures.

❖ I am going to put money into my business, and it will be successful.

❖ My salary is negotiable, and I have the right to do so.

❖ I am entitled to ask for as much money as I deserve.

❖ Saving money comes easily to me.

❖ I am going to establish a deadline for goals today.

❖ My debt has no power over me.

❖ I take pleasure in the money I earn.

❖ I have skills and creativity that will help me live a happy and prosperous life.

❖ I will not waste money on frivolous purchases.

❖ I am capable of setting reasonable objectives.

❖ I am committed to obtaining financial security.

❖ I will end the financial insecurity that has plagued my generation.

❖ I'm confident that with my adjustments, I will attain my financial goals.

❖ I enjoy saving money.

❖ I won't spend money that I do not have.

❖ I will achieve financial independence.

7

SHE BIRTHS ROYALTY

"It is easier to build strong children than it is to repair broken men."

— FREDERICK DOUGLAS

Motherhood is such an amazing gift. For many women, it's the complete essence of womanhood. Even women who don't want to have kids (and that's not a problem) will agree that there is something in us that just cries out to nurture something or someone. However, although motherhood can be one of the greatest blessings in the world, it's also one of the most challenging vocations.

The day I gave birth brought me so much joy. When I looked at my sons, I saw a level of perfection and purity which I had never experienced before. Even though I was filled with a great sense of pride, my feelings were dampened within a few months by the reminder that their lives may not be as I envisioned because of the melanin of their skin. I knew life could be tough for them because of their race.

Sometimes I stayed up late wondering about the kind of conversations I would need to have with them concerning race and the realities of the world. It hurt to think about how long it would be before I would have to burst their bubble of innocence. As mothers, the world gives us so many reasons to worry about our children but being a Black mother in America is an entirely different beast. It's a difficult endeavor to teach our children about racial awareness without instilling fear. And it's an even loftier task to help them view their Blackness as a privilege instead of a burden.

Ultimately, the mantle of being a mother is a glorious privilege. And being a Black mother is something to be celebrated and respected. There are so many dangers we must protect our children from that it is truly a divine undertaking. There are the horrors of the streets, police violence, racial profiling, and educational disparities, just to name a few.

If we look from the vantage point of the African-American narrative, Black mothers spent centuries nursing and rearing their owner's white children. However, this never seemed to translate into an appreciation and admiration for our amazing ability and competence to nurture and mother our own children.

Due to the systems set in place to keep us down, such as a judicial system created to keep our partners imprisoned, neighborhood redlining which resulted in educational disparities, and low employment opportunities, we have often found ourselves in environments that lack the necessary resources for raising children. And yet, when we call upon governmental services created for everyone, only WE are labeled welfare-queens. We are shamed for seeking out resources that can assist with providing for our children. Furthermore, we are degraded and called "baby-mamas," and our parenting style is at times seen as harsh.

Despite all of this, we are more than a symbol of strength for losing our children to white supremacist violence. We are not just heroes because we advocate for better maternal-pregnancy outcomes. No, we are so much more than this. We are divine bearers of life. We are endowed with the power to create Kings and Queens.

So don't stop fighting for your kids. Don't stop fighting for your right to be a mom. You're never alone. Whenever you get discouraged, remember that you are molding a King and Queen and in time, you'll see the rewards.

Now, I have some amazing motherhood affirmations that will help you. I remember them whenever I get tired or face a hurdle in my journey of motherhood, and I know they will help you too. When life and society attack your motherhood, repeat these affirmations to yourself. Wake up every day and repeat these words. They will strengthen and enable you to hold on and keep going.

So, just as we've been doing, look in the mirror and repeat these words to yourself:

❖ **I am the perfect mother for my children.**
❖ **I am the mother that my children need.**
❖ **I am a great provider and protector of my children.**
❖ **I am raising strong Kings and Queens.**
❖ **I am instilling confidence and self-esteem into my children.**
❖ **I am teaching them to love their identity.**
❖ **Although my motherhood is often portrayed as something to be endured, I find joy.**

❖ I reject the images of welfare reliance and tropes of Black mothers as militant and uneducated.

❖ I find great joy in reading books to my children that speak of their Black heritage, culture, and pride.

❖ I educate my children on the contributions of their Black predecessors.

❖ I am a nurturer.

❖ My feminine presence radiates a feeling of peace, safety, and comfort in my home.

❖ The love I have for my children is fierce and unequaled.

❖ I take pride in applying hair butter to my child's head and watching their little curls form tendrils.

❖ I am a great mother.

❖ I am a great role model for my children.

❖ I have a vision for my children.

❖ Each day I learn and grow as a mother.

❖ I will never be perfect, but I am the perfect mother for my children.

❖ I celebrate my heritage by playing the rhythmic beats that leave them entranced by the music of their ancestors.

❖ I am aware and present in my child's life.

❖ I am raising children that will contribute to society in powerful ways.

❖ I am not a "baby mama," I am a mother.

❖ Raising children alone does not make me a bad mother.

❖ I instill healthy values into my children.

❖ I have healthy boundaries between me and my children. If I am not well, my children cannot be well.

❖ If I need it, I will seek help for my family. This is not shameful.

❖ My time is the most important resource I can give to my children.

❖ The joy I cultivate in my family is not dependent upon my income.

❖ The home I create now will be the home my children create later.

❖ I will break generational curses.

❖ I model the home that I want my children to have.

❖ I exemplify the relationships I want my children to have.

❖ I instill worth into my child.

❖ I praise my children daily.

❖ I empower my children to rise above their mistakes.

❖ I create a safe space and environment for dialogue and open communication.

❖ I do not need permission to feel glorious as a mother.

❖ I am doing my best as a mom.

❖ I am the best mother for my children; I was born to be their mother.

❖ I am important in the lives of my children.

❖ By allowing myself to be happy, I inspire my family to be happy as well.

❖ Mistakes and setbacks are stepping stones in my motherhood journey because I learn from them.

❖ Happiness is my choice.

❖ Only I can give my children a happy mother.

❖ I am a blessing to my children.

❖ I am doing an amazing job.

❖ I am my child's lifelong teacher.

❖ I trust my maternal intuition.

❖ I will talk about myself the way I want my children to talk about themselves.

❖ I am learning to be a better mother with each new day.

❖ Today I will notice the positive aspects of my motherhood.

❖ I will take care of myself to be a good mother.

❖ I am grateful for my ability to create life.

❖ I see the value in the mundane duties of motherhood.

❖ I deserve to put my feet up and relax.

❖ I will be kind to myself.

❖ I gain confidence as a mother daily.

❖ Being a mother makes me feel beautiful.

❖ Being a mother has shown me how strong I am.

❖ I am raising adults who will contribute to the good of society.

❖ Motherhood reveals my strengths to me.

❖ I will play with my children today.

❖ I will never miss opportunities to make memories with my children.

❖ I will not allow domestic duties to infringe upon the time and attention I devote to my children.

❖ The decisions made by other moms do not need to dictate mine or how I feel about myself as a mother.

❖ There is no such thing as "just a mom."

❖ My children will remember the time we spent together, not what they were given.

❖ I love my children even on the days I don't particularly like them.

❖ My children love me and are thankful for me, even when they don't say it.

❖ I will show my children what it means to take care of oneself.

❖ I will pour into myself so that I can parent from a place of rest and happiness rather than exhaustion and bitterness.

❖ I will not worry about small details today.

❖ I will turn away from judgment today.

❖ My children care more about my attention than my flaws.

❖ I do not expect to be a perfect mother.

❖ I will have realistic expectations for myself and my version of motherhood.

❖ I embrace the here and now.

❖ I am calm and peaceful under pressure in the home.

❖ My children will feel accepted and loved unconditionally by me.

❖ Asking for help does not mean I'm a failure as a mom.

❖ My imperfections today are not important.

❖ As I teach my kids today, I will also be open to the lessons they can teach me.

❖ Every challenge I face makes me stronger as a mother.

❖ I will show my children how to advocate for kindness and justice.

❖ I am more than enough.

❖ I take care of my body, mind, and soul.

❖ I am unwavering in my love for my children.

❖ I parent with love and respect, not anger.

❖ In my journey to motherhood, I will be patient and gracious with myself.

"There is no influence so powerful as that of the mother."

— SARAH JOSEPHA HALE

8

IT'S THE SOUL THAT NEEDS THE SURGERY...

"It's not the load that breaks you down; it's the way you carry it."

— LENA HORNE

We have all experienced hardship, disappointment, and adversity that left emotional wounds in our hearts. Perhaps, you've gone through so much in your life that you don't even think it's possible to heal from the pain. And as Black women, we endure more than our fair share of heartache. We are confronted with hate, discrimination, and abuse from society. And what hurts, even more, is when we suffer these things from the people we love.

It is far too common that Black women suffer the consequences of a broken home. What about the pain and trauma that comes with the loss of a parent? How many Black women have had to go through life without the love, protection, and encouragement of their fathers or the warm touch of a mother? Here's a poem I wrote many years ago that I believe tells the story of Black women who have gone through life without the presence of a father. I entitled it "Daddy's Little Girl."

Daddy's Little Girl

Daddy never came to count and tickle the toes on my feet,
Never did my father's swooning neck peer into my crib,
making sure I was asleep,
As I skipped through the house in my pink little dress,
He wasn't there to call me his little princess,
Where was he when strange men entered my room in silence,
These foreigners mommy said she loved stripped me of my
innocence,
Daddy never heard my cries, my knight in shining armor
never came,
But who was to blame... when my brother had the same
nightmares, or so I called them,
When he screamed hysterically at the foes upon him,

I wanted to be rescued from the fear and horror,
To lay my head on daddy's warm chest, feeling the security of
his core
I wished he could wrap his hands around my waist
As we danced slow and steady to his smooth pace,
Never was I thrown high into the air awaiting the catch of
the two strong arms,
I only fell time and again without a hand to pull me from
harm,
The stubble from his face never prickled my soft cheeks,
Not once did he kiss me goodnight and tuck me snugly into
my sheets,
The bedtime intruders developed me quickly into a tween,
But what was I between? Was I a woman or a piece of meat?
Daddy couldn't praise the new fullness of my frame,
To tell me the beauty of my kinky, curly mane,
I wished he told me how perfectly my nose spread,
That my eyes were shaped like almonds, that my skin was
caramel red,
I felt ugly, insecure, worthless, and alone,
Until asked to prom, by a guy I'd barely known,
The special night came, dressed in all my fancy array
Daddy didn't tell me that I looked amazing, that I was
special, that I should wait,
Wasn't there to ask questions; he couldn't drill my very first
date!
Like a bride on her wedding day, he didn't give me away,

So I gave myself away, away to moral decay,
My body was the way to the love that I deserved,
No longer was there part of me that I preserved,
As I stand on the corner, I wonder if daddy would ask:
Where's the rest of your clothing, why are you wearing that
mask?
But now, it's all too late, said and done
After the time is up, I'm still abandoned,

Now with a little creature growing inside,
I wonder how I'm going to provide without a shield by my
side,
What do I tell my baby boy about how to be a man?
When a man is nothing more than flowers and one-night-
stands,
What do I say to my baby girl when she asks what "daddy"
means?
Without a man to cuddle her gently and tell her she's a
Queen,

My mother surpassed the duties of her role by more than ten
times,
But she could never fill the shoes my father left behind,

The aching in my soul has never ceased a single day,
I wished my hero came, the man to take me away.

Sadly, this is the story of many of us. Society has severely underrated the impact a father has in the life of a woman. It breaks my heart whenever I see young Black women hurting themselves emotionally by giving away their preciousness to undeserving men who prey on their vulnerability. Sometimes, we get upset and wonder why a fellow Black woman who should know her worth will stay in a chronically toxic relationship. But she's never heard a man call her beautiful except the one who slept with her. She's never heard a man tell her she's worth it or that she is whole and complete. A daughter gets her first sense of identity and self-worth from her father. So when that love and approval of a father is absent in a woman's life, she tends to look for it subconsciously in other men. This is because that little girl in her is still looking for a father.

Even though trauma can be a destructive and damaging part of our lives, there are many women who have overcome the pain from their pasts. I'd like to talk about an exceptional Black woman who went through a great deal of trauma throughout her life.

In the winter of 1954, a baby girl was born to a teenage mom, who worked as a maid while her father was in the Armed Forces. Shortly after birth, her mother went north, and the child spent the first six years of her life in rural poverty with her maternal grandmother. Her grandmother was so poor that the young girl had to wear dresses made from potato sacks and many children in her neighborhood made fun of her.

Sadly, the girl's grandmother was abusive toward her, and when she was six, she moved back with her mother. Unfortunately, her mother didn't treat her any better than her grandmother did.

Her father didn't come back into the picture until she was nine years old, which is when she lived with him temporarily. While she stayed with her father, she was sexually molested by a cousin, an uncle, and a family friend. And sadly, she suffered this abuse until she ran away at the age of 13. By the time she reached 14 years of age, she found herself pregnant, only to have her child die after being born prematurely.

She eventually went back to live again with her mother and was transferred to a high school in a rich suburban neighborhood. Whenever she rode the bus on her way to school, she would be reminded of how poor her family was as she was often accompanied by Black kids who were the children of her classmates' servants.

She wanted to feel like she belonged, and she was deeply hurt seeing other kids in school being able to spend freely while she had to struggle to eat. So, she started stealing from her mom so she could spend like her richer classmates. But her mother found out and sent her to live with her father permanently.

Although her father was a strict man, he encouraged her to do better in school, and she did. In fact, it was while she was living with her father that she got noticed by a radio station at the age of 17, and her journey to media stardom began.

Oprah Winfrey, the richest Black woman in the world is a powerful example of a Black woman who endured many painful experiences while growing up; from severe impoverishment to bullying, sexual abuse, the loss of a child, and living in multiple broken and unstable homes. She was truly dealt a tough hand but found a way to overcome the obstacles she faced in her past. Winfrey seized the open doors before her and leaned into her craft while creating a life that many are inspired by. Despite her challenging child-hood, she has displayed unmatched resilience and has served as an incredible example of how to overcome trauma. Even though her story is exceptional, she shouldn't be viewed as the outlier, but as someone, we can emulate.

There are so many of us who have suffered trauma, affecting us in ways that haunt us to this day. The reality is that most of us are not equipped to deal with the scars before they do significant harm, spreading into all areas of our lives. That's when seeking help comes in.

Look, I know many of us feel queasy about going to therapy and seeing a mental health professional because of the stigma surrounding therapy, especially in the Black community. But the bottom line is that it's about your well-being. Sis, there is absolutely nothing wrong with seeing a therapist, especially when you have realized that the wounds from your past are more than you can bear. I know that you might prefer finding solace in friends and family, but sometimes, we need the expertise of a professional. A therapist can walk you through your past hurts, and painful memories, and start you on the path toward healing.

Because the truth is, sometimes, we develop destructive patterns of behavior due to damaging experiences in our past. And when these patterns aren't dealt with, we can pass them on to our kids. That's when we begin to see things like generational curses that create ripple effects, plaguing entire families. But you shouldn't allow your past to affect the beautiful and glorious future ahead of you. Your past doesn't have to determine your future. Just like the Lena Horne quote at the beginning of the chapter, your pain doesn't have to break you. It's not about the pain; it's about the way you deal with it.

Another wonderful tool that can help you through healing is affirmations. And since we've been on this journey, you know how beneficial they can be.

Make sure you look in the mirror when you say these affirmations. Don't be afraid to cry or get overwhelmed. It's all part of the healing process, love.

Now, when you're ready, repeat these words aloud:

❖ I cultivate a healthy body and a tranquil mind.
❖ Every day, I work toward healing my deepest pains and overcoming them.
❖ I validate and treat my emotional wounds.
❖ I am patient with myself during my healing process.
❖ I am radiant and attract happiness in my life.
❖ I respect my feelings and accept them as they are.
❖ I forgive myself for the mistakes I have committed.
❖ I am learning to love myself more and more every day.
❖ I have the power to heal inside and out.
❖ Happiness is my strength. It heals my wounds and pains.
❖ I give myself enough time to heal.
❖ I deserve inner peace.

❖ I let go of past happenings that do not serve a worthy purpose.

❖ I refuse to harbor resentments and my energy is intended for joy.

❖ Contentment is my right, and I will pursue it.

❖ I will release emotional baggage and I will never let it define me.

❖ My soul is full of love for myself.

❖ I feel grateful for the life that I have.

❖ I am not a victim but a survivor.

❖ I have the ability to let go of the emotional weight that prevents me from enjoying my life.

❖ I choose to live a full and fulfilling life.

❖ Nothing weighs me down; my spirit is light.

❖ My pain will heal.

❖ I am committed to my healing journey.

❖ I will overcome any emotional obstacle.

❖ I have unconditional love and respect for myself.

❖ I do not dwell on my problems but prefer to find solutions.

❖ I voice my thoughts and validate my feelings.

❖ I have the power to heal my deep cuts and wounds.

❖ I trust the process of healing and harnessing happy thoughts.

❖ I live in the present moment and invite happiness into my life.

❖ I give myself enough time to heal from within because I know I deserve it.

❖ I am gentle with myself and never push hard to achieve things that are not worthy.

❖ I accept my sadness and inner pain, because it's okay to feel like that.

❖ Every hurtful situation is an opportunity to heal emotionally and evolve spiritually.

❖ My inner wounds do not define my existence. I am worthy of attracting happiness and peace of mind.

❖ Things happen for a reason, as they always teach you something.

❖ I made mistakes because I am not perfect. And that's okay.

❖ Self-hatred does not serve me.

❖ I am a good person, and I am growing daily.

❖ I am letting go of all the anger and anxiety.

❖ I deserve true love from people.

❖ I choose to forgive, and I choose to be free.

❖ I treat myself with love and compassion.

❖ I am striving to have a peaceful inner space.

❖ I am choosing to forgive myself.

❖ I have forgiven all who have given me immense pain and agony.

❖ I free myself from intrusive thoughts, doubt, and fear.

❖ I reject situations and people that take away my inner peace.

❖ I accept my imperfections with ease and grace.

❖ I choose to let go of the past.

❖ I am ready to give life another shot.

❖ Something good is coming to me.

❖ I am going to be okay.

❖ I do not allow anxiety and worries to take away my peace.

❖ I meditate to let go of anxious thoughts and disturbing feelings.

❖ I forgive myself for not being perfect.

❖ I honor who I am.

❖ I am not the woman I used to be.

❖ The pain from my past has shaped me into a strong and wise woman.

❖ I have learned from my mistakes, and I forgive myself.

❖ I will no longer hold onto the shame from my past.

❖ I will forgive those who have hurt me.

❖ I will not repay evil for evil. I will not hurt those that have hurt me.

❖ I will not project my pain onto others.

❖ My past does not define me.

❖ I am more than the negative comments people say about me.

❖ I will not be ashamed to seek professional help. I

will break the cycle of the stigma behind therapy in the Black community.

"You may not control all the events that happen to you, but you can decide not to be reduced by them."

— MAYA ANGELOU

9

TRUE LOVE IS WORTH WAITING FOR

"What's meant for you will find you. You won't have to chase it, force it, settle or fight to keep it alive. It won't break you, hurt you or question you. It will heal you, understand you & be patient with your trust. To attract it, fully let go of all thoughts that do not promote your growth."

— EBRAHIM ASEEM

After I graduated from college, I felt the pressure more than ever to settle down and start a family. I had a good job and was headed to law school, but I wasn't in a relationship, and in a way, that negated all my other successes. So, I started going on dates and eventually met a guy I liked. We dated for about 6 months, and I even told him I loved him. But now, when I look back, I almost feel a little embarrassed for stooping so low. Not because he was a bad guy but because in reality, I deserved so much more. At the time, I was just drawn to the fact that he was intelligent and completing his master's at a prestigious college.

However, there were so many ways that I was bending over backward to make the relationship work. I planned a lot of our date nights, and I even paid for a majority of them by sparing him the embarrassment of sneaking my card to the waiter when we were with other couples. He didn't drive, have a license, or even a car. And when it came to getting a job, he said he just couldn't find one even after I revised his resume and encouraged him to go to career fairs. I thought he was my future, and yet I was pouring far more into the relationship than he was.

Sometimes, we may think that we are in love with somebody, but truly, we are in love with the idea of that person. We are in love with their potential. We invest so much time and energy into trying to shape the person into who we want them to be, we stroke their egos, and eventually, due to all of our hard work, they may even get the confidence they need. But if we give them a million chances after mistakes, we are not their woman; we are their mom.

As Black women, we love hard. We serve and give our last in relationships, but sometimes it's to a fault. In the name of loyalty, we give our all to non-reciprocal partners who meet none of our needs. This is NOT loyalty; it's desperation. We are so desperate for love and so afraid of being alone that we are willing to settle for a warm body instead of a quality partner who is committed to loving us. We all have to grow in relationships, but if we truly cared about our partner's growth, we would stop stunting their growth by rewarding their half-efforts with our amazing presence. We give them beautiful children, cook, clean, provide financially, chauffeur them around and even pump gas. We build them up and encourage them to pursue their dreams, and we are often left with nothing to show for it. Of course, not all of our romantic relationships fail, but the statistics tell a sobering story especially if we look at the high rates of single motherhood within our community. We are certainly not the leading racial group for nuclear families.

I'm sure that many of us have felt this notion that Black women are "leftovers." Remember that scene in the movie, "Daddy's Little Girls," where Idris Elba's character was asking Gabrielle Union why she was always going on those blind dates her friends set up for her? She made a statement that painfully struck me. She said, "Black men don't wanna date Black women." For some reason, in the dating pool, we're left behind. And what's even sadder is when we are overlooked by Black men, not because of an attitude problem, unlikeable personality, or a lack of beauty, but by virtue of just being a Black woman. It's painful to be rejected by a man and what pours more salt on the wound is being rejected by a man within our race. Since we are caught at the intersectionality of being Black and a woman, we are already at the bottom of the totem pole and marginalized on so many levels. And when we look to find a mate that would be the most likely to understand our unique struggles and perhaps would appreciate us the most, we are rejected by them. "Our" own men don't even want us. And it hurts. It hurts every time we get called "ghetto," "lacking class," "trashy," "triflin," and "nappy-headed" by them. We're seen as women who do nothing but "tear a brother down." But we aren't like that. We are SO much more.

Let me shock you with some statistics that show how much we are disadvantaged in the dating pool. Here's a statement made by Shantel Buggs, a Ph.D. candidate in

Sociology at the University of Texas[1]: "Society tells us that Black women are hypersexual but also more masculine than other women [...] and that they are physically less attractive. All of this centers on Euro-centric beauty standards, which privilege those who are white or are white adjacent in appearance — things like lighter skin, light-colored eyes, thinner noses, and certain jawline shapes. So, when we see Black women having a harder time, part of it has to do with beauty standards, and part of it has to do with the ways people are socialized to imagine how Black women behave inside and outside of relationships."

Many men have fetishes about Black women. They don't want to date Black women, but they want to sleep with Black women. So, in their minds, Black women are good for just one thing. While this reality is painful, it doesn't mean we should allow it to shape our identity. You are not any of these stereotypes, and you need to stand up against these labels.

As Black women, we are deserving of reciprocal love. We can't keep tolerating the BS. We must raise our standards. WE have to see ourselves as the Queens that we are. We have to stop pouring out more of ourselves when we know we see the red flags and inconsistency. We can't let the fear of being lonely cause us to try and trap a man with a baby or make compromises that destroy every aspect of our lives. Let's start only pouring energy into partners who are reflections of the Queens we want to be.

So, ladies, like we've been doing throughout this journey, we're going to affirm ourselves. We're going to restructure our mindset about our worth as it pertains to our love life and relationships. So, look in the mirror, place your hand on your chest and repeat these words:

❖ **I am the whole package.**
❖ **I deserve a partner who respects me and listens intently.**
❖ **I practice healthy boundaries when pursuing romance.**
❖ **I am worthy of love and deserve to receive love in abundance.**
❖ **My relationships are positive and offer the highest good to all of those affected by them.**
❖ **I don't need to do anything to deserve love.**
❖ **I choose to believe in true love despite my experience.**
❖ **I am ready for love to change my life.**
❖ **I am genuinely open, vulnerable, and trusting with my loved ones.**
❖ **My love is a precious gift, and I have the power to choose when, how, and to whom to give it.**

❖ I am meant to be with someone who is not only interested in me but is also intentional with me.

❖ I do not give away my love cheaply. My love deserves to be earned.

❖ I will no longer make excuses for partners who don't want to be in my life and who need to be excused from my life.

❖ I am strong enough to let go of a toxic partner.

❖ I love those around me, and I love myself.

❖ I attract loving and caring people into my life.

❖ The door to lasting love is open to me.

❖ The love I seek from others needs to be cultivated within me first.

❖ My love is beautiful, intense, and passionate.

❖ Even if I am hurt, I choose to offer love and compassion because it is the right thing to do.

❖ I will not be shamed or swayed into compromising my character.

❖ I will not tolerate abusive language or behavior by myself or others.

❖ My happiness is determined by me and not my relationship status.

❖ I am loveable.

❖ I am open to receiving love.

❖ I love myself deeply and fully.

❖ I am here to experience love.

❖ I am worthy of celebrating myself.

❖ My love is unconditional.

❖ Every day I am grateful for how loved I am and how much people care about me.

❖ I open my heart to love and know that I deserve it.

❖ I pursue only loyal, supporting, and loving relationships.

❖ I am becoming the woman that will attract a quality partner.

❖ I have as much responsibility in a relationship as my partner.

❖ I am attracting my dream partner, the perfect person for me.

❖ I am capable and deserving of a long-lasting relationship.

❖ I am confident, self-assured, and full of charisma.

❖ I will practice self-love and heal from past hurts before entering into a new romantic relationship.

❖ I will not project past baggage onto a new relationship.

❖ I am not afraid to abandon an unhealthy relationship.

❖ I have the courage to address aspects of the relationship that are problematic for me.

❖ I am not afraid of conflict, as it allows me to live a freer and truer life.

❖ I deserve to be happy in my relationship.

❖ I will never give up on finding true love.

❖ I create a safe space and environment for dialogue and open communication.

❖ I am choosing instead of waiting to be chosen.

❖ I deserve wholesome love and affection.

❖ I am worthy of a healthy, loving, wholesome relationship.

❖ I deserve to be happy in my relationship.

❖ Every day, I will continue to create the foundation of a happy and loving relationship.

❖ I deserve passion in my relationship.

❖ I choose to love hard and wholeheartedly, and I deserve someone who loves me in the same way.

❖ Happiness begins with me and me alone.

❖ I have the power to create my happiness.

❖ I let go of my past relationships and look to the future.

❖ I choose to only think positively about love.

❖ It's not a race to get into a relationship.

❖ I am not behind in life if I am not in a relationship.

❖ I am never desperate in my pursuit of love.

❖ My body was created for commitment.

❖ I am willing to put in the work to find a partner for life, not a partner for the night.

❖ I have all of the qualities I need to make a good partner.

❖ I love who I am, and I am ready to be loved intentionally.

❖ **I am ready to share my kindness, affection, and beauty with a committed partner.**

❖ **I am excited to give the best of myself in a relationship.**

❖ **My love is much more than sensual.**

Now, if you're already in a relationship or marriage, here are some affirmations that will help to strengthen the bond between you and your partner. We're going to say it the same way we've been doing with the others. So repeat these words aloud:

❖ **My partner shares in my joy but is not its source.**

❖ **My partner and I both deserve to love and be loved.**

❖ **My partner and I deserve a long-lasting, happy, satisfying relationship.**

❖ **I am conscious and considerate of my partner's needs.**

❖ **I am in a loving, committed, strong relationship.**

❖ **My love for my partner grows stronger each passing day.**

❖ **My partner and I accept each other's strengths and weaknesses.**

❖ **I am always supportive of my partner, just as they are supportive of me.**

❖ I feel comfortable and safe whenever we are together.

❖ The love that I have for my partner is stronger than our fights and misunderstandings.

❖ I am happy and content with the relationship I have with my partner.

❖ I am grateful for all the things that my partner does for me.

❖ The grass is never greener on the other side; it's greener where I water and tend to it.

❖ Love is a choice, and I choose to love my partner every day as they choose to love me.

❖ I choose to have a forgiving and forbearing heart towards my partner.

❖ I am not blind to my partner's faults, but I do not focus on them.

❖ My partner and I give our relationship the time and attention it deserves.

❖ My relationship grows stronger every day.

❖ I choose to always fight fair in my relationship.

❖ I choose to remain faithful to my partner and choose to let them know if we need repair.

❖ I accept my partner with all their strengths and weaknesses.

❖ I acknowledge that my partner is not perfect, just as I am not perfect.

❖ I listen with an open heart and a loving ear.

❖ I choose to always put in my best in my relationship.

❖ I choose to love my partner with an understanding heart and an open mind.

❖ I wholeheartedly accept my partner's flaws and always leave room for encouragement and growth.

❖ I love my partner through thick and thin.

10

HEY, SOUL SISTA

"You have to fill your bucket with positive energy-and if you have people hanging around you that are bringing you down and not lifting you, whether that's your, "boo" or your best friend - you have to learn to push these people to the side."

— MICHELLE OBAMA

One thing I love about the movie, "Why Did I Get Married" and its sequel is the amazing friendship between the women in the film. Sheila, Angela, Diane, and Patricia portray what friendship should be like between Black women. The way they constantly stood up for each other through thick and thin was just amazing. The way they supported Patricia through her terrible divorce despite her faults was truly something to see. They weren't just friends, they were sisters, and that's how it should be. We should never be alone, and I love to see Black women with solid, unbreakable friendships.

Healthy relationships are essential for everyone. Your friends and the people you choose to spend your time with could be the most influential people in shaping your life and perspective.

And don't give me that, "I don't need any friends" or "girls are a bunch of snakes," thing. You know as well as I do that there are amazing, beautiful, honest women out there. Some women feel they don't need friends because of past betrayals and hurt and I can totally understand that, but don't rob yourself of the richness of having beautiful female friendships. I can't count how many times my friends have been by my side to get me through a rough season in life and the thing is that you don't need to have a lot of friends. But, it is important how you pick your friends, and I'm telling you that when you find a group of women that you can rely on, it's beyond wonderful.

The fostering and maintaining power of female friendships has been studied extensively. These findings suggest that friendships play an important role in women's general health and happiness, from their awkward teenage years to their golden years.

Good friends can help you see things from different perspectives; although women receive affection and support from their relationships, [1]LYSN psychologist Breanna Jayne Sada believes that a female friend can provide a fresh perspective in times of need. In addition, a female friend can be an outsider looking in when it comes to relationships, delivering honest counsel that you may not want to hear, but that can favorably affect your actions.

Sada pointed out that while a friend's honesty can be brutal, at least you know you're getting the truth. Female friends can act as sounding boards, listening to your ideas and thoughts before telling you what they think. Following a talk with them, you can feel more secure and supported. Sada even went on to say that studies have indicated that women who have great connections have a better chance of surviving breast cancer than those who are socially isolated! Allow that to soak in for a second; female friendships can help you live longer. How crazy is that?!

Okay, okay. I know I'm getting sciencey, but one last fun fact. Female friendships can also prevent depression in elderly women. According to an article in

Psychology Today,[2] female friendships can help older women deal with sadness. It was pointed out that friendships are about more than just having fun and playing games. They are essential for one's physical and mental wellbeing, as loneliness and isolation are significant contributors to depression. While your children and husbands may not understand the challenges of aging, your dearest friends will; whether it's menopause or deciding whether to change careers or retire, there's always a struggle.

So, you've seen that even science recognizes the benefits of having solid friendships. Look, Sis, I know the world is rife with nasty people who seem wonderful at first, and when you let them into your life, they betray you. I have had such experiences, and they affected my perspective on female friendships, but the truth is that we need women around us who we can rely on. We need that one person that we can call in the middle of the night and cry our eyes out without fear of condemnation. I love seeing solid female friendships that have lasted the test of time. I want to have that too and we all need to have and be that kind of friend.

So, don't shy away from making friends with your fellow Black women. The bottom line is that we need each other. Our struggles are unique and there are certain things we experience that only a Sista would understand. I love seeing Black women coming together to encourage and strengthen one another. I have tasted the benefits of having such friendships, and I want you to have the same. There's so much we can learn as a community of Black women, even across generations.

So here are some good friendship affirmations that will help to reset your mindset about female friendships. We're going to recite them like we've been doing. So, every morning, go to the mirror and say these words out loud:

❖ **My time is valuable, and I spend it in memorable and impactful ways with the people closest to me.**
❖ **I am honest with my friends, and they are honest with me.**
❖ **I have healthy expectations of my friendships.**
❖ **I choose my friends and I am proud to associate with them.**
❖ **I let go of people who treat me poorly.**
❖ **My friendships value my work, my attention, and my time.**
❖ **I am a great friend.**
❖ **My friends are dependable and trustworthy.**
❖ **My friends respect me.**
❖ **I am a loving and caring friend.**
❖ **I bring out the best in others.**

❖ My friends bring out the best in me.

❖ I don't allow friends to pressure me into compromising situations.

❖ I will not settle for less than the best from myself and others.

❖ I will surround myself with positive people.

❖ I invest my time and energy into those that appreciate me.

❖ I cannot fix everyone's issues, but I will always be there for my friends.

❖ I feel safe with my friends and family.

❖ My friends make me laugh, and that gives me joy.

❖ My best friends make the best company.

❖ All my friends are lovely people.

❖ My friends and I encourage one another in all our efforts.

❖ I can rely on my friends for support, emotional or otherwise.

❖ I will make my friendships beautiful and fulfilling.

❖ I love making friends that I genuinely admire.

❖ I am ready to make new friends, and now I will attract the perfect friends for me.

❖ Every day, I allow positive and amazing people to enter my life.

❖ Everyone in my circle is a loyal and trustworthy person.

❖ I am comfortable making new friends.

❖ I refuse to allow jealousy or envy to prevent a great friendship.

❖ I can be authentically me and still have amazing friendships.

❖ I am not afraid of making new friends daily.

❖ I am strong enough to maintain long-lasting friendships.

❖ My friends accept me for who I am.

❖ I am loyal to my friends.

❖ Any toxic people in my life are better left behind.

❖ I won't chase after people who will let me down.

❖ I trust myself and my friends.

❖ I reject friends that are emotional vampires and leech off my energy.

❖ Loving myself lets me love my friends genuinely.

❖ I refuse to gossip about my friends.

❖ I don't lend money to friends that are financially irresponsible.

❖ My friends are multi-dimensional.

❖ I embrace a diverse group of friends.

❖ I don't need to be perfect to have perfect friends.

❖ A perfect friend does not have to be a perfect person.

❖ I am not ashamed of any of my friends.

❖ I have healthy and deep conversations in my relationships.

❖ I reject perpetual liars and welcome authentic people.

❖ I set healthy and balanced boundaries.

❖ I thank my friends for being themselves.

❖ I am proud of my circle of friends.

❖ I am vulnerable with people who can be entrusted with my heart.

❖ My friends have vision for me, and I have vision for them.

❖ My friends get to be themselves all the time, as they should be.

❖ My friends sacrifice for me, and I do the same for them.

❖ I am good enough for my friends to love me.

❖ My friends are my comfort in dark times.

❖ My circle of friends will only keep expanding.

❖ It's okay to outgrow certain friendships.

❖ All of my friendships are reciprocal.

❖ My friends hold excellent values.

❖ I respect the difference between friends and acquaintances.

❖ I let my friends know that they matter to me.

❖ I have the right to choose friendships that benefit me.

❖ There are opportunities to make friends everywhere I go.

❖ I always make the right friends at the right time.

❖ New friendships are exciting to me.

❖ I attract nice people.

❖ The friends I make are like-minded people.

❖ I know exactly how my best friend will be because I strive to be that kind of person.

❖ Each of my friendships brings me joy.

❖ I can be honest with my friends, just like they're always honest with me.

❖ When my friends need me, I'll be there for them.

❖ My friends give me the energy I need.

❖ I strive to be a supportive friend.

❖ Being a supportive friend to others gives me purpose.

❖ I make sure to cherish all my friendships.

❖ All my friendships bring about feelings of warmth and care.

❖ I look for friends who empower me as I can do the same to them.

❖ I can say no to friends, and they'll understand.

❖ I value the companionship of all my friends.

11

EYES ON THE PRIZE!

"For me, becoming isn't about arriving somewhere or achieving a certain aim. I see it instead as forward motion, a means of evolving, a way to reach continuously toward a better self. The journey doesn't end."

— MICHELLE OBAMA

A successful woman is self-assured and knows exactly what she wants. She is a risk-taker and a fighter; she understands what she has to offer, is conscious of her flaws, and has learned to work around them. Does this describe you? We all possess the characteristics of a successful lady. You just have to channel them more often!

A lot of women think that being a woman is all about being a great wife and an exceptional mom. It has a lot to do with that, but that's not all there is to life. A woman isn't just meant to be a wife and mother; you should have dreams and ambitions. You should have a purpose; you know, something that keeps you up at night, something that gets you excited. If you're single, don't spend all your time waiting for a man to come and sweep you off your feet. There is so much you have to offer to the world, so much you have to give. This is the time when you should be getting out there and trying out things to discover what you're good at. This is the stage where you should be setting goals and making things happen in your life; this is the time when you should be chasing dreams and actively working on yourself.

And again, if you're married, you're not just meant to be a mom and a wife because life doesn't end after marriage or after having kids. I know developing your interests may be harder because you have more responsibilities, but you can still live your life to the fullest. Life is so big! Don't give up on your dreams and ambitions. Keep pushing until you have the life you want, the life you truly deserve.

You might be thinking, "is it possible for my life to be more than what I see? Is it possible for me to be more than I am?" The answer to these questions is a resounding yes! But it all depends on you, Sis. You just need to take things one step at a time. So think about your goals and your future. Every day, when you wake up in the morning, remind yourself that you were made for so much more. Press forward every day towards those goals. Strive to be the best of yourself every day.

Let me tell you a little story about myself. You see, growing up as a child, I wanted to be a lot of things. I had a very vivid and rich imagination. Somehow, I knew I was special and meant to do something wonderful in the world. Then I grew up, and you can say life happened. As I mentioned in earlier chapters, after college I worked at a law firm while I applied for law schools across the country. The day I received my acceptance letter, I was overjoyed. I could so vividly envision myself defending the voiceless before a court, saving young Black juvenile defenders from a future of life behind bars. I could just see the letters, "Esq." after my name. I went through that first semester of my schooling with such zeal and passion. I was doing it; I was on my way. But underneath it all, my body was attacking me. With each passing day, I felt sicker and sicker. My body was fighting against me, and I didn't know why. The aches and pains were eventually accompanied by debilitating fatigue. And eventually, I couldn't do it anymore. I had to drop out, and I was devastated. Despite this major disappointment, I reasoned that no one who finds great success tells a perfect story. A little diversity is what makes it powerful, right?

So I mustered up enough faith to apply again, and within 6 months I had been accepted into another great law school. With a year of recovery under my belt I felt ready to pursue my dream again. But still, with no diagnosis, and no plan for maintenance, the host of symptoms quickly returned. I fought against my unknown illness for many months with anything I could think of, with treatments like acupuncture, herbal teas, cupping, and juicing. I even went so far as to become a vegan. But to no avail, my body was not having it. My good grades, praise from professors, and overall aptitude for law were no match for my health. So I did what I had done before, I left, but this time for good. My dreams of becoming a lawyer were over, and I didn't know where to turn. I was crushed, felt directionless, and devoid of purpose. If I wasn't going to be an attorney, what was I destined to be? I used to be convinced I could change the world, but I wasn't as sure of myself anymore. I thought that perhaps great things were only meant for specific kinds of people; people who actually had both the talent and ability to go after their dreams.

I developed a sense of inferiority complex and I felt I didn't have what it took to be successful. So there I was; I woke up, ate, worked, and slept. Waiting. Not really living. Merely existing. But I began to see women like me who were taking charge of their lives despite their varying limitations, and I received a kind of strength from their stories. If they could do it, why couldn't I? That thing you think is stopping you may not be a real obstacle at all. There are people who have less than what you have, and they have done so much with it. I was so glued to my weaknesses that I lost sight of my strengths, as they were the only thing I was focused on. At that time, if someone asked me what I was good at, my answer was always, "I don't know." So I saw them as excuses for not leaving my comfort zone and they were the reasons why I didn't strive for more.

I'm glad that with the help of friends, family, and God I snapped out of all of that because it's not a fun place to be. You may be like a diamond in the rough. Precious and priceless but needing refinement. But that refinement comes through actively chasing your dreams. It comes through choosing to live an abundant and bold life. It comes through setting goals and actively working towards achieving them. And don't say you can't do it; you've been saying that for years. You can do it and you will.

Don't think about the mistakes you've made and how much time has passed because that won't matter in the long run. And don't think about your age. I have seen many Black women in their fifties go back to school and get outstanding degrees. I have also seen Black women in their seventies set up very successful businesses.

One beautiful thing that will happen to you when you press toward your goals and plans for the future is that when you eventually succeed, you will look back on this time and thank yourself for making the right decision. You will look back and marvel at the amazing woman you have become.

Sometimes, achieving our goals doesn't even take as much as we believe because a lot can happen in six months. A whole lot can happen in a year. With diligence and determination, you can completely transform yourself and your life in just twelve months. Thankfully, these qualities are inborn in Black women. We have proven countless times that we are capable of more than we are given credit for so take advantage of your God-given strength. Go back to the drawing board. Revisit those goals and dreams you've set aside and start moving!

Remember that the choices you make today will determine your future. So, start making the right choices. A huge part of where you are today is a direct result of the decisions that you have made in the past. Perhaps they were wrong decisions, and that's nothing to feel bad about, Sis. I have made some bad decisions in my life. We can't change the past, but we can change the future, and it starts with the decisions you make today.

"It's interesting how nothing changes day by day, but when you look back, everything has changed," says a popular adage. Whatever happens, you'll be a year older in a year. What can you accomplish today with your goals to make looking back on today feel completely different and rewarding?

Now, here are some great affirmations to help you on the journey to achieving your goals and planning for your future.

Say these words out loud:

- ❖ **I am capable of embodying all my desires.**
- ❖ **I strongly acknowledge my capacity to succeed.**
- ❖ **I believe something amazing is about to happen to me.**
- ❖ **I allow passion to guide me in all the actions I take.**
- ❖ **Everything will work.**
- ❖ **I choose happiness in all the paths I walk on.**
- ❖ **My mind is devoid of obstructions and open to possibilities.**

❖ I am developing into a promising version of myself.

❖ I look for positivity in every situation.

❖ My desires are pursued by the unlimited faith I have in myself.

❖ If I place my mind on something, I will achieve it.

❖ I have extreme confidence in my proficiency.

❖ I have the aptitudes which are essential to reach my goals.

❖ I can handle any obstruction that lies in my path.

❖ I have enormous courage lying within me all the time.

❖ I have the determination to keep moving ahead in life.

❖ My goals are more important than any fear that pulls me down.

❖ I have enough faith in my endurance.

❖ My strength is greater than my fears.

❖ Today I face everything with tremendous vitality.

❖ I have the determination to walk the path I have set for my dreams.

❖ I might fail, but I will never give up.

❖ I learn from every experience.

❖ I can create the life that I have dreamt of.

❖ I am directed toward my goals and will never quit.

❖ I am in control of whatever I wish to do in the future.

❖ My circumstances do not decide my future.

❖ My decisions are the only thing that determines my future.

❖ My reality is determined by my positive energy.

❖ I will manifest anything that I focus on.

❖ I am living a life dedicated to my goals.

❖ I will never let the purpose of my striving fade away in difficult times.

❖ I cherish the life which I am creating every day.

❖ I seize every opportunity in front of me and boldly advance toward my goals.

❖ My failures are merely learning opportunities never regret.

❖ My goals are the manifestations of my heart's desires.

❖ I am living a life that is aligned with my highest truth.

❖ I have immense faith in myself even in the face of adversity.

❖ My goals are achievable.

❖ I navigate my path with grit and grace.

❖ I see prosperity in my future.

❖ I attract positivity and abundance.

❖ I will never neglect my responsibilities in pursuit of my goals.

❖ I am worthy of dreaming big.

❖ I refuse to shy away from working hard to achieve my goals.

❖ I have gratitude for what I already have, and I will keep striving for what I do not have.

❖ My dreams will turn into reality because of my strong and purposeful endeavors.

❖ I am taking actions that push me closer to attaining my future goals.

❖ I am calm, composed, and open to improvement.

❖ I am confident my efforts will make my dreams come true.

❖ I am open to seeking help from people who are more knowledgeable and can illuminate my path.

❖ I am optimistic about my future.

❖ I devote my time to planning, researching, and preparing myself for my goals.

❖ I have impactful ideas, and I can implement them powerfully.

❖ I network with people to gain insight and glean from their experiences.

❖ I will sharpen and hone my skills every day.

❖ I will associate myself only with like-minded people whose positivity encourages my dreams.

❖ My spirit prompts me every day to make greater efforts to realize my dreams.

❖ I am completely aware of my strengths and weaknesses and work on them daily.

❖ I have the power to unlock my fullest potential.

❖ I am grounded and working silently towards my goals.

❖ I am a proactive person.

❖ I will stop procrastinating and choose to act in the present, to make my future better.

❖ I take action instead of simply talking about pursuing my goals.

❖ I keep track of my time and understand its importance.

❖ I am becoming more productive with every passing day.

❖ I start all my projects early and finish on time.

❖ Every day I am more passionate and energized to continue working on my goals.

❖ I maximize my efforts and success.

❖ I get the job done.

❖ I will never give up on my goals just because it is tough to achieve them.

❖ I push myself toward the highest levels of happiness and success.

❖ I am free from anything that causes self-doubt and negativity.

❖ My future doesn't just happen, it's the result of my choices.

❖ Lazy is not a part of my vocabulary.

❖ I recognize and avoid distractions.

❖ I am proud of my journey.

❖ I celebrate every success along the way to achieving my dreams.

❖ My past does not prevent me from enjoying future successes.

❖ I don't make excuses because they stifle my imagination.

❖ I am creative and determined so I will be successful.

❖ I will create opportunities for myself when none are presented to me.

❖ I am the facilitator of my success.

❖ I determine the outcome of my future.

12

EVEN QUEENS REST

"We must reject not only the stereotypes that others hold of us but also the stereotypes that we hold of ourselves."

— SHIRLEY CHISOLM

Have you ever felt guilty for taking a break even when your entire body is screaming for you to rest? I have. Many times. But why? Who said that Black women don't deserve rest? Why do we get dogged when we decide to take a break? When other women do it, it's called self-care, and they are applauded for it. But when we do it, we are tagged as lazy.

It reminds me of the slavery era when Black slaves were worked to the bone and punished for attempting to rest or slow down. Black people were seen as strong and resilient, which is a major reason why they were put to work in the fields. As a Black woman, you are incredibly powerful, but you must know your limits, or you will wear yourself out.

I remember the first time I broke down horribly; it was just a few years ago. I had been overworking myself for weeks at a stretch and I knew I needed rest because my body was screaming for it. My brain was shutting down and refusing to go further, but I didn't listen. For some reason, I thought I hadn't really done enough to deserve rest. I simply didn't want to disappoint those around me.

But what I failed to understand is that if anything happened to me, the work would still go on even if it had to be done by someone else. So I kept on pushing until my body pushed back. I was sick for a long time. Although I recovered, I wasn't really the same after that. It seemed my body intentionally lowered its threshold for stress and would signal me anytime I was coming dangerously close to that mark.

Listen, Queens. You deserve to rest. You work so hard in and out of the home. Don't let society make you feel guilty for taking breaks. It's so beneficial to your overall health and I'll show you how in a bit. But I want to get rid of that mindset that you have to work like a hamster on a wheel all the days of your life.

If you've ever wondered why we are sometimes so stressed, irritated, and touchy, it's because we don't rest. Our cortisol levels get shot through the roof. And it's not very surprising when we look at the world we live in. We feel we have to overcompensate and do twice as much as what other people are doing just to get by. We have to work harder and smarter all the time. Yet, we are called lazy and harassed for "abusing the system" every time we ask for help. Society sees us as unproductive when we begin to cry for help, but we are not readily celebrated for the work we do. We are not lazy; we are just tired. Tired of carrying burdens too heavy for our shoulders, tired of carrying the responsibility of our families all alone, tired of trying to be the best daughter, wife, mother, employer, entrepreneur, and CEO, and tired of trying to please society.

But we can't keep going like this. It has gotten to a point where we need to fight for our right to rest. We are not lazy for slowing down and taking breaks. No, we are not. If you've been feeling guilty about wanting to slow things down, don't. You deserve it. It's your right.

You've done so much. It's not easy to be you and to have to do the things you do.

You see, rest helps your body to heal. The human body is designed to perform a succession of quick sprints, and this is why taking a break, even if it's only for a few minutes, can provide you with the energy you need to get through the day. Work, physical activity, or mental tension should all be interrupted by breaks. These moments of reprieve improve mental health, creativity, productivity, stress reduction, mood improvement, and even strengthen relationships. Rest allows your body to engage its healing powers and return to balance. This is the time when your body can heal and rebuild itself.

On a different note, did you know that you are inherently more creative after you take time to rest and relax? You can replenish your reserves by taking time off. The quiet can encourage reflection, helping you to break past creative barriers. As a result, you'll find yourself solving more open-ended challenges by gleaning new insights or coming up with novel ideas.

Additionally, proper rest also increases productivity. When you're tired, your brain, like the muscles in your body, becomes less functional. Resting sharpens your intellect, which is one reason why Mondays are often loaded with high-priority chores or meetings. When you return from the weekend, you will be able to work more efficiently since you took time off.

Now, rest is only significant when it is done on purpose. So I'm going to share a few ways you can intentionally incorporate rest into your daily schedule.

When life gets hectic, and your to-do list grows longer, plan relaxation like a meeting or appointment. Yes! Create basic daily habits that remind you to rest; it will make resting a breeze, and you won't feel guilty for doing it.

Another practice I have is just taking some time off to meditate on the things I have in my life, such as the things I'm grateful for. While we are so immersed in the hustle and bustle of today's world, we forget to be thankful. While we're chasing things we don't have, we can fail to appreciate what we do have. When was the last time you just sat down to think about the many blessings you have? When was the last time you looked at your beautiful babies and just smiled with content-ment? When was the last time you were grateful to have good friends in your life? Most individuals focus their gratitude on the "big" things; but instead, be apprecia-tive of the "small" things. Frequent and positive thoughts like these will boost your mood and increase your overall contentment.

Here are some of my bedtime affirmations. Ideally, you should say them as you're winding down. So, just like we've been doing, say these words aloud:

❖ **I am grateful for the abundance that is currently in my life.**
❖ **I do not blame anyone for where I am at in life. I refuse to give them that power over my life.**
❖ **Rest is a privilege I'm entitled to.**
❖ **Rest is a healthy part of my life.**
❖ **I am not lazy because I rest.**
❖ **I am thankful for today.**
❖ **I feel calm and at peace.**
❖ **I am in control of my thoughts, and I choose positive ones.**
❖ **I choose calm. I choose peace.**
❖ **I let go of my responsibilities of the day.**
❖ **I let go of worry.**
❖ **I let go of what I can't control.**
❖ **I release anything that didn't go well today.**
❖ **My to-do list will wait for tomorrow.**
❖ **Nothing will disturb my peace unless I let it.**
❖ **I let go of the past and the future. I focus on the present moment.**
❖ **I let go of tense thoughts.**
❖ **I am still and calm.**
❖ **I breathe deeply and slowly.**

❖ I am grateful for the simple and profound joys of
the day.

❖ I am grateful for my bed, my room, and my body.

❖ I permit myself to do nothing.

❖ I am enough and I've done enough today.

❖ I forgive myself for any mistakes made today.

❖ I forgive others that made mistakes today.

❖ I am allowed to feel good at the end of the day.

❖ I release the anxieties and stress of the day.

❖ I am grateful for the lessons that today brought.

❖ Peace and happiness are my priority as I finish
my day.

❖ I worked hard today and deserve to rest. There is
nothing more I can do tonight.

❖ I permit myself to sleep deeply.

❖ My body feels heavy and relaxed.

❖ My body and mind need rest and rejuvenation to
function well.

❖ Sleep and rest are essential to my success.

❖ I did my best today, and now I rest.

❖ I embrace rest and welcome sleep.

❖ My sleep will be calm and peaceful.

❖ My mind and spirit are still and tranquil.

❖ I relax my head, face, neck, arms, stomach, legs,
and feet. I let them sink deeply into the bed.

❖ I empty my head of racing thoughts. I let them
float along, or I tuck them away for another time.

❖ I allow myself to let go of the day.

❖ I am grateful for the moments with my kids today.

❖ I am grateful for the opportunity to care for my family.

❖ I did my best today with my children, and that is enough.

❖ No one needs me now. It's time to be kind to myself and relax.

❖ I am the best mom I can be when I permit myself to rest.

❖ I am a better mom when I make my sleep and well-being a priority.

❖ I withdraw from the outside world when I need time for self-care.

❖ I am satisfied with what I have accomplished today

❖ I rest with tomorrow in mind.

❖ I am proud of my work. I am anxious about nothing.

❖ I rest for myself, and my family.

❖ I rest so I may always give my best.

❖ Tomorrow is a new day with new possibilities.

❖ I use my time purposefully, and that includes time off.

❖ My rest is my responsibility, and I will protect it.

❖ In my journey to success, I can take a rest.

❖ I will listen to my body when it feels off or tells me to slow down.

❖ I am worthy of repose.

❖ I will let go of all of my worries and empty my mind of all negativity.

❖ I have done enough today, and I am at peace with my efforts.

❖ I am grateful for rest because I can recharge and heal.

❖ Every hour of my day is purposeful and productive, even when I rest.

❖ I will let go of all stress so I may have moments of respite.

❖ I will meditate until my mind drifts into positivity.

❖ I refuse to let thoughts wander into negativity.

❖ I have control over my racing thoughts.

❖ My thoughts flow toward gratitude and relaxation.

❖ I will focus my thoughts on singular aims.

❖ I welcome warm thoughts and happy dreams.

❖ My worries and responsibilities can wait until tomorrow.

❖ I rest to renew my spirit.

❖ I release my frustration and anxiety into the universe.

❖ I exhale the pain and grief from my day.

❖ I do not hold onto emotional weight.

❖ I do not let people disturb my peace.

❖ My downtime is precious.

❖ I love slowing down.

❖ I rest today for a better tomorrow.

❖ My dreams are a place of solitude and peace.

❖ My rest is a requirement.

13

THE BIRTH OF A QUEEN

"*Marriage is hard. Divorce is hard. Choose your hard. Obesity is hard. Being fit is hard. Choose your hard. Being in debt is hard. Being financially disciplined is hard. Choose your hard. Communication is hard. Not communicating is hard. Choose your hard. Life will never be easy. It will always be hard. But we can choose our hard. Pick wisely.*"

— UNKNOWN

Let's face the facts. As Black women, we hold unique intersectionality. We are not only viewed as the lesser gender, but we are also seen as the inferior race. Many systems are set in place to continue to oppress, devalue, and stifle our progress. And these are systems that we will undoubtedly continue to fight for until we see the change that we are looking for.

However, this is not the scariest reality. What is more frightening than the systems in place is how we have enslaved ourselves within our own minds. It's time to unlock our minds and set ourselves free from centuries of self-doubt, fear, and insecurity. Because what we do have control over is our thoughts and actions and how we choose to walk in our divine womanhood and Blackness. This cannot be taken from us, BUT it has to be cultivated.

What I love about the quote at the beginning of this chapter is that it places the responsibility of change directly on us. It strips us of all ability to make excuses and place blame on the many variables of life. Only YOU have the power to change the outcome of your life. Only YOU are in charge of your life and how your life will turn out. Life is hard. It has always been hard. And it will always be hard. However, every day we get to choose the kind of hard that we want to live with. We have full autonomy over ourselves. We can always choose how we respond to life and the curveballs it throws us.

In this book, there have been many affirmations shared. However, it would be unrealistic to assume that you would recite all of them daily. Therefore, I would encourage you to compile your favorites from each section into a manageable list that you can recite every day. Try this for 30 days and enjoy the positive effects that manifest in your life.

So with these affirmations and the little tips given in this book, will you choose to take control of your mornings, finances, motherhood, career, goals, friendships, relationships, and health? Will you actively work on your self-esteem and confidence and begin to see yourself as the beautiful woman you are? Will you work on healing emotionally and learning how to rest? Or has this amazing journey been for nothing? The decision is yours, Sis, and I know you will make the right choice. As long as you have breath in your lungs, you still have the opportunity to become the Queen you desire to be.

Congratulations! You've made it to the point where you're well on your way to becoming the new woman you desire. If you believe this book benefited you in any way, please leave a review on Amazon. Reviews will help this book reach other Black women who may need to be reminded of how amazing they are. Let's get this book into the hands of as many Black women as possible. Imagine if all Black women knew their divine worth and value. Isn't that a lovely thought?

If you liked this book and would like to listen to it, you can find it on Audible by searching for "The New Black Woman."

14

BONUS CHAPTER – THE SCIENCE OF AFFIRMATIONS

"It's the repetition of affirmations that leads to belief. And once that belief becomes a deep conviction, things begin to happen."

— MUHAMMAD ALI

How often have you undermined your efforts due to negative thoughts or feelings of guilt or shame? If you answer more than once, you've already answered too many times. This is a common practice. Many of us suffer from negative ideas that impair our self-esteem, confidence, attitude, and mood. However, the issue with these is that they frequently become self-fulfilling prophecies.

What exactly does that imply?

It means that what we think about ourselves creates our reality: our beliefs influence our actions, and our actions influence our fate. As a result, our negative views become more entrenched, and we withdraw from the important things in life, dragging our aspirations, relationships, careers, and friendships down the drain.

But is it possible to end this vicious cycle?

Yes! Without a doubt! This chapter's objective is to enlighten you about positive affirmations and to assist you in transforming your self-doubts and negative ideas into motivating daily affirmations.

WHAT ARE POSITIVE AFFIRMATIONS?

Affirmations are positive remarks that can assist you in overcoming self-defeating and negative thinking. You can start seeing improvements if you repeat them frequently.

We use them to motivate ourselves to make positive changes in our lives or increase our self-esteem and confidence. If you are constantly thinking negatively, using daily affirmations to replace these bad habits with positive ones is one of the most powerful strategies for transforming your mind and life!

THE SCIENCE BEHIND POSITIVE AFFIRMATIONS

We now know that positive affirmations are a self-help approach for combating negative, unhelpful ideas and boosting self-confidence. Is this method, however, effective? Is it scientifically supported?

Yes, positive affirmations work, and science backs them up. Studies[1] have shown positive affirmations to activate areas of the brain connected with self-related processing and reward. Positive affirmations can also assist in the creation or restoration of self-competence.

To grasp how positive affirmations function and get the most out of them, you must first learn about neuroplasticity, or the brain's ability to reorganize itself.

Although being one of the most advanced and complex structures in the universe, the human brain can get confused about distinguishing between reality and imagination. This particular flaw serves as a source of self-assurance.

To clarify, repeating affirmations daily aids your brain in forming a mental image of the goal you're aiming for or the version of yourself you want to be.

When you build a mental image, it engages the same portions of your brain that would be triggered if you encounter the goal you're attempting to achieve in real life.

Simply said, by repeating positive affirming statements, you train your brain to accept them as true. As a result, you'll be better prepared to take the *action* necessary to achieve your goal.

Why is the word 'action' emphasized, you're wondering? That's because positive affirmations only work if you do something to achieve your goal. It's unrealistic to believe that repeating a few words may make a difference in your life. Affirming assertions should be seen as the first step toward change, not as a change in and of themselves.

Let's use an example to put all of this into context. Assume you're a private individual who dislikes answering personal questions; when such inquiries are asked, you become irritated and unable to respond without coming across as harsh.

So, in this case, you would repeat a positive affirmation such as, "I can stay calm and composed when I'm angry or agitated."

By repeating the following affirmation, you may begin to develop the practice of breathing deeply into your diaphragm, which can have a calming impact. You could find yourself doing grounding techniques as well. To get the most out of daily positive affirmations, you must combine affirming remarks with actual action.

Claude Steele's self-affirmation theory is one of the most well-known theories about positive affirmations. Its origins can be traced back to the 1980s.

According to this view, threatening information activates the self-affirmation process by confronting our sufficiency or integrity. The goal of self-affirmations is to re-establish our sense of self as adequate, moral, competent, good, coherent, stable, capable of making significant decisions, and so on.

All of this is accomplished through rationalization, explanation, and action. Positive affirmations are mostly used to deal with threats to our self-image rather than the problem itself.

Threats aren't the only reason to use self-affirmations as they also assist us in creating a positive self-identity narrative. This is a flexible view of ourselves as daughters, sons, friends, parents, students, neighbors, etc. We measure success in different ways based on each of these positions.

THE SELF-AFFIRMATION THEORY

We've already mentioned neuroplasticity[2] to demonstrate that positive affirmations are entirely based on research and have nothing to do with magic, but is that all there is to it in terms of science? What does positive affirmation have to do with psychology?

Claude Steele, a social psychologist and retired professor at Stanford University, championed self-affirmation theory[3] in the 1980s, driving it to the forefront of social psychology research.

Self-affirmation theory is a psychological theory that explains how people cope with experiences and knowledge that threaten their self-concept or self-identity[4]. According to self-affirmation theory, we can sustain self-integrity, which is linked to self-efficacy, by positively affirming our essential values and beliefs.

And self-efficacy is our perception of our ability to deal with danger to our self-concept without jeopardizing our essential values or beliefs. Our perception of our capabilities to respond dynamically and uncompromisingly to situations or knowledge challenges our self-concept.

We contribute to establishing a universal paradigm about our identity by exercising self-affirmation, and within the context of the global story we've built, we must characterize ourselves as moral and adaptable.

This also allows us to look at notions like success and happiness from various perspectives, allowing us to better adjust to changing circumstances.

Additionally, according to self-affirmation theory, a person's identity should not require them to strive for perfection or greatness. Rather, individuals should aim for proficiency in aspects of living that are important to them.

The last piece of the jigsaw in the self-affirmation theory is sustaining self-integrity. It's performing in ways that align with our values and beliefs, and it's a principle worth praising and recognizing.

Since it was popularized, the self-affirmation theory has attracted much interest from neuroscientists, prompting them to perform investigations and research to determine if it changes brain activity.

One study[5] used MRI evidence to show that neural connections in the ventromedial prefrontal cortex strengthen when a person practices self-affirmation. This area of the brain is responsible for self-related cognitive processing and positive appraisal.

According to another study[6], self-affirmation can change the brain's response to frightening information, making it self-relevant and valued. Self-affirmation is not a fanciful new-age activity.

The authors of a 2014 review of studies on positive affirmations came to a handful of key conclusions:

- Self-affirmations assist us in dealing with situations that endanger our integrity, performance, or personal development.
- Most of them revolve around rethinking our essential personal ideals;
- Affirmations given at the right time can aid in education, health, and relationships.
- The advantages can last for months, if not years.
- Once they trigger a pattern of adaptive potential and a positive feedback loop between the individual and the social system, they can achieve long-term advantages.

But, if this isn't enough to persuade you, I can become even more "sciencey."

In 2016, a team of scientists set out to discover whether self-affirmations are linked to an underlying neurological mechanism.

The study's participants were randomly assigned to two groups and given a task; one group received affirmation after completing it, whereas the other did not. An MRI machine was used to monitor their brain activities during the experiment.

The findings indicated that when we receive affirmations, the activation of various brain networks increases. These areas of the brain are also in charge of processing self-related data and values, implying that affirmations are all about solidifying our positive identities.

BENEFITS OF POSITIVE AFFIRMATION

Repeating self-affirming mantras and phrases might be beneficial, but you must remember that action is required. Affirmations are little more than words if they aren't followed through on. Some of the advantages of positive affirmations are as follows:

Reduced negative thoughts: Because most of your thoughts are subconscious, using positive affirmations helps you become more aware of your ideas and feelings. This empowers you to stop destructive thought processes in their tracks.

Increased happiness: When you practice self-affirmation, you become more mindful of what makes you unhappy. As a result of your newfound understanding, you'll be able to associate yourself with the things that make you happy.

Increased gratitude: In the middle of the day-to-day rush and bustle, the tiny things in life frequently go unappreciated. Self-affirmation can assist you in focusing on and being appreciative of the simple things that you may take for granted.

Good thinking reinforced: Practicing self-affirmation can positively impact the way you think and your view on life. Studies[7] have also shown that optimism lowers the risk of developing cardiovascular disease, including strokes and heart attacks.

Reduced resistance: A person who practices self-affirmation regularly is less likely to react negatively to frightening facts or messages. Instead, they'll react to make a positive difference.

FAMOUS PEOPLE WHO HAVE USED THE POWER OF AFFIRMATION TO CHANGE THEIR LIVES

While some may think of affirmations as a "new age" innovation, the principle of positive thought has been used throughout history. It has resurfaced as a self-development and well-being technique in the early twentieth century. While affirmations are not usually embraced in popular circles, there are several case studies of affirmations being used successfully to enhance health, promote motivation, and attract riches, as seen below.

Napoleon Hill

Philosophers and natural healers have employed positive thought to achieve the desired result throughout history. Napoleon Hill, the author of "Think and Grow Rich," published in 1937, is the most well-known proponent of affirmations in modern times.

Hill found the keys to success by studying over 500 successful men during his time, and the book is still popular today. The stories had one thing in common: the men were nearly single-mindedly focused on a goal and used all of their mental energy on it. Most significantly, the men in issue were certain that they would achieve their objectives. Hill claims that articulated, defined desire and journaling, creative imagery, and affirmations were the keys to their success in his book.

Napoleon Hill is widely considered the modern father of affirmations and positive thinking. People all across the world devoured his book, which had sold more than 20 million copies by the time he died in 1970. Although Mr. Hill's teachings are largely geared toward attracting riches, the ideas he teaches can be applied to any goal, including excellent health.

Louise Hay

Louise Hay is a more modern pioneer in affirmations for physical healing. Louise was a victim of rape and violence as a child, was forced to drop out of high school due to teenage pregnancy, and eventually divorced. Louise was ultimately diagnosed with cervical cancer after enduring so much suffering; nonetheless, she refused conventional therapy.

Louise did some soul-searching and concluded that the sexual and emotional abuse she had received as a kid and the failure of her marriage had paved the way for her sickness. She had been a member of the Church of Religious Sciences a few years before, and she had adopted their belief that physical ailment was caused by mental and emotional distress. Louise conducted classes on utilizing affirmations to cure oneself. She used the same treatment on herself and was able to get rid of her cancer.

Louise proceeded to publish "You Can Heal Yourself," a modest book that became highly successful. She identified several ailments and the possible emotional or mental trauma that caused them. Louise also created healing affirmations that she repeated daily to heal emotional scars and, as a result, the body. Louise went on to write several books that have helped millions of individuals all around the world recover through the use of positive affirmations and self-love.

Louise launched Hay House Publishing, which publishes books in the health, self-help, and transformative categories from authors who are truly dedicated to their calling. Despite being in her eighties, Louise is still actively leading the world's largest publisher of transforming books, radio shows, and live events. Her continued good health in her later years is a tribute to the efficacy of Louise's recommendations. In addition to her other responsibilities, Louise sends out a daily affirmation to help others achieve optimal health and prosperous life.

Bernie Siegel, M.D.

Dr. Bernie Siegel is a world-renowned metaphysical healer and a luminary in the area. Dr. Siegel developed a unique level of awareness and sympathy for those he cared for as a surgeon who had worked with terminally ill patients, veterans, and children.

Dr. Siegel uncovered a wealth of information from his interactions with terminally ill patients. Many of the patients blamed their illnesses on a lack of love and fulfillment in their lives; many of them had let insecurity, fear, and trauma dictate their lives, preventing them from reaching their full potential. Furthermore, Dr. Siegel's work with youngsters revealed several cases of family dysfunction, inattentive or unloving parents, and peer pressure, all of which played a significant role in their diseases.

Dr. Siegel released "Love, Medicine, and Miracles" in 1986, based on his newfound knowledge. Dr. Siegel detailed the healing and peace he experienced in patients who were given a second shot at love and acceptance in one of the first books of its kind written by a medical doctor. Dr. Siegel coined the phrase "reparenting" to describe a procedure in which patients, both young and elderly, were given the love and nurturing they lacked as children. Dr. Siegel provided a sense of serenity and improved health to many people by acting as a surrogate father.

Dr. Siegel's work with patients included a lot of creative imagery, therapeutic drawing interpretation, and healing affirmations. Dr. Siegel's goal was to rewire the brain and subconscious mind to establish a more balanced and healthy environment, allowing the body to repair itself. He is still giving talks about the healing power of love and positive thinking.

Dr. Siegel is still giving talks about the healing power of love and positive thinking. "A Book of Miracles - Inspiring True Stories of Healing, Gratitude, and Love," his most recent book, is a collection of his thoughts gleaned from 25 years of transforming healing work. Dr. Siegel also runs a cancer support group and has written many poems and healing affirmations that he freely shares with health seekers worldwide.

Lissa Rankin, Ph.D.

Dr. Rankin, a relative newcomer to transformative health and wellness, is bringing greater attention and a new viewpoint to the self-healing hypothesis. Dr. Rankin, a board-certified gynecologist, became disillusioned with the excessively sterile and patriarchal healthcare system, which pressured doctors to perform even when overworked and ill while treating patients as statistics to be served as swiftly as possible.

Dr. Rankin quit her managed care practice after considerable soul searching to pursue a quieter existence, which included moving to the country and focusing full time on her other vocation as an artist. During this period, Dr. Rankin started on a spiritual journey that included healing affirmations, allowing her to recover from some of the trauma she had experienced during her medical profession and remove some of the limiting beliefs that had tormented her since she was a child.

Even though she was in better condition and feeling more fulfilled, Dr. Rankin felt compelled to return to medicine. She accomplished so by establishing the "Owning Pink" Medical Center, which aimed to integrate feminine compassion into health care by empowering patients to connect with their inner guidance and gain the confidence to heal themselves.

In this vein, Dr. Rankin created the "Whole Health Cairn," which is a visual representation of a stack of rocks, each representing a different aspect of your life. Relationships, profession, spiritual practice, sexuality, and other topics are covered, with the physical body represented by the uppermost rock. According to Dr. Rankin, if any of these core areas are out of balance, the body will be unstable, and sickness will occur. However, if you cure these regions, the rest of your body will do the same.

Dr. Rankin went on to develop the Owning Pink online community, which helps people tap into their healing potential. Dr. Rankin is a strong proponent of affirmations in healing therapy and sends out a daily email with uplifting and therapeutic messages.

Denzel Washington

Denzel Washington, an A-list Hollywood actor, also owes his meteoric rise to affirmations. With the support of his positive thinking, he overcame his drinking addiction and all other issues that were preventing his mind and body from reaching greater achievements. He began to believe in himself and eventually rose to the top!

Jennifer Lopez

According to the megastar, her day isn't complete unless she spends at least 15 minutes practicing affirmations. She has always stated that affirmations have helped her achieve success and that they are what keep her grounded. Affirmations, she claims, help her stay strong and positive in a vicious and difficult job.

NOTES

5. BLACK AND DROP-DEAD GORGEOUS

1. https://www.google.com/amp/s/face2faceafrica.com/article/
how-cornrows-were-used-as-an-escape-map-from-slavery-
across-south-america/amp

6. GET THAT COIN

1. https://www.google.com/amp/s/www.brookings.edu/blog/up-
front/2020/12/08/the-black-white-wealth-gap-left-black-
households-more-vulnerable/amp/

9. TRUE LOVE IS WORTH WAITING FOR

1. https://www.thestar.com/life/2017/03/21/racism-and-match-
making.html

10. HEY, SOUL SISTA

1. https://welysn.com/articles/5-reasons-why-female-friendships-
are-vital-for-you/
2. https://www.psychologytoday.com/us/blog/mindful-
anger/201802/are-female-friendships-the-key-happiness-in-
older-women

14. BONUS CHAPTER – THE SCIENCE OF AFFIRMATIONS

1. https://www.ncbi.nlm.nih.gov/pmc/articles/PMC4814782/
2. https://www.healthline.com/health/rewiring-your-brain
3. https://www.sciencedirect.com/science/article/abs/pii/S0065260106380045
4. https://www.verywellmind.com/what-is-self-concept-2795865
5. https://www.ncbi.nlm.nih.gov/pmc/articles/PMC4814782/
6. https://www.ncbi.nlm.nih.gov/pmc/articles/PMC4814782/
7. https://www.ncbi.nlm.nih.gov/pmc/articles/PMC6777240/

Made in the USA
Columbia, SC
22 August 2022

65827148R00102